ॐ

# Aitareya

# UPANISHAD

## Essence and Sanskrit Grammar

Ashwini Kumar Aggarwal

जय गुरुदेव

ISBN13: 978-81-945212-5-9 Paperback Edition
ISBN13: 978-81-945212-6-6 Hardbound Edition
ISBN13: 978-81-945212-7-3 Digital Edition



Title: Aitareya Upanishad
SubTitle: Essence and Sanskrit Grammar

Printed and Published by
Devotees of Sri Sri Ravi Shankar Ashram
34 Sunny Enclave, Devigarh Road
Patiala 147001, Punjab, India

https://advaita56.weebly.com/
The Art of Living Centre

https://www.artofliving.org/

2nd April 2020, Ram Navami, Lord's Meditation on Beauty
On 2-4- 2011, India crowned Cricket World Cup Champion
Vikram Samvat 2077 Pramathi, Saka Era 1942 Sharvari

1st Edition April 2020

जय गुरुदेव

# Dedication

## Sri Sri Ravi Shankar

who lives the ideal principles
of Lord Rama
and restores Ram Rajya

# Preface

Ram Navami is a powerful and pressing occasion for man to turn to Meditation. Amongst all the human beings through history, Lord Ram is depicted as the *perfect individual*, the one who lived his entire life on fundamental humane principles.

Meditation is not esoteric, neither is it vague, distant, hard or impractical. Meditation is in fact the direct and most effective tool for man to attain oneness within and union with divinity.

| Veda | |
|---|---|
| Mantra Verses (Samhita) | Brahmana Verses |
| | Brahmana<br>Aranyaka<br>Upanishad |

Adi Shankaracharya's masterly commentary on eleven Upanishads is the de facto standard for Vedanta. These eleven have been named the principal Upanishads. Though it is said there are 1180 Upanishads written over a period of a thousand years, actual manuscripts available as of now are 108 only.

A chart that lists the eleven Upanishads commented on in detail by Sankara.

| Rigveda | Samaveda | Shukla Yajurveda<br>Krishna Yajurveda | Atharvaveda |
|---|---|---|---|
| Gives the fundamental laws of creation | Gives the intrinsic harmony within creation | Gives the specific design, administrative and governing principles for a family or a nation | Gives the specific ritucharya and dinacharya for an individual |
| **Aitareya** | Kena<br>**Chandogya** | Ishavasya<br>**Brihadaranyaka**<br>Katha<br>Taittiriya<br>Shvetashvatara | **Mandukya**<br>Mundaka<br>Prashna |
| प्रज्ञानं ब्रह्म | तत् त्वम् असि | अहं ब्रह्म अस्मि | अयम् आत्मा ब्रह्म |

Four great illuminating statements or mahavakyas are listed above with their corresponding Upanishads in **bold**. Aitareya's mahavakya occurs in the 5th section towards the end - Prajnana Brahman - प्रज्ञानं ब्रह्म ॥ 3.1.3

Remember that Vedic Sanskrit text cannot be literally translated into English. Thoughts form and words sprout in deep meditation when guided by a living master.

Rig Veda = Rigveda Samhita + Rigveda Brahmana

Aitareya is one of the earliest Upanishads and is attributed to sage Mahidasa Aitareya. It consists of five sections, viz. sections 21 to 25. These sections form the 4th, 5th and 6th chapters of the 2nd part of the Rigveda Aranyaka.

As of today the Rigveda Brahmana is available in two recensions named Aitareya and Kauṣitaki, of which the Rigveda Aranyaka is a subset.

For

- the young student the मन्त्र Samhita verses
- the householder the ब्राह्मण Brahmana verses
- the retired the आरण्यक Aranyaka verses
- the sannyasi the उपनिषद् Upanishad verses.

Young Student = one who is yet being cared for by parents.
Householder = one who is in the thick of earning, raising a family, or actively engaged in society.
Retired = one who is out of the grind and living on savings.
Sannyasi = one who is free in mind and light at heart.

These four phases are not separated in time or by age. These may occur in any order in a man's life, sometimes concurrent, sometimes distinct. One may have the Sannyasa experience earlier and get thrown into the Householder struggle later. It happens. The key point to understand is that these are states of the mind, heart, intellect and emotion, and one's relationships in society.

Aitareya ऐतरेय means the one whose mother is named इतरा Itara. Mahidasa means the one who serves महि = भूमि = Mother Earth. It is said this Upanishad is by Mahidasa Aitareya.

Using simple yet elegant words, the Rishi narrates the story of creation from the Big Bang onwards. The complete paraphernalia for its functioning is described, also the biology of man's birth. An incisive statement is made that points to the undeniable fact "Opposite Values are Complementary in Nature". Its mahavakya is **prajñānaṃ brahma,** i.e. **Consciousness = the Divine = the Supreme.**

Giving the example of sage Vamadeva who attained enlightenment, a devotee is inspired and empowered to embark on an inward journey…

## Blessing

“राम मने क्या ?– राम मने अन्तर ज्योति आत्म ज्योति ।
हमारे भीतर जो प्रकाश है, हमारे हृदय मे जो प्रकाश है वहि राम है ।

राम हमेशा हमारे हृदय मे जगमगा रहे हैं ।”

Sri Sri Ravi Shankar
Live from Bangalore Ashram 2nd April 2020

## Acknowledgements

On the occasion of Ram Navami, Sri Sri conducts online live “Ram Meditation” at 12 pm noon IST.
https://www.youtube.com/watch?v=rVxV_AeizLE

## Cover Photo Credits

https://pixabay.com/photos/shower-of-sparks-light-steel-wool-3115784/
Image by Sandra Wagner from Pixabay

# Table of Contents

## Prayer

### शान्तिपाठः

ॐ वाङ् मे मनसि प्रतिष्ठिता । मनो मे वाचि प्रतिष्ठितम् । आविरावीर्म एधि। वेदस्य म आणीस्थः ।श्रुतं मे मा प्रहासीः। अनेनाधीतेनाहोरात्रान् सन्दधामि । ऋतं वदिष्यामि । सत्यं वदिष्यामि । तन्माम् अवतु । तद् वक्तारम् अवतु । अवतु माम् । अवतु वक्तारम् अवतु वक्तारम् ॥
ॐ शान्तिः शान्तिः शान्तिः ॥

śāntipāṭhaḥ
oṃ vāṅ me manasi pratiṣṭhitā । mano me vāci pratiṣṭhitam । āvirāvīrma edhi । vedasya ma āṇīsthaḥ । śrutaṃ me mā prahāsīḥ । anenādhītenāhorātrān sandadhāmi । ṛtaṃ vadiṣyāmi । satyaṃ vadiṣyāmi । tanmām avatu । tad vaktāram avatu । avatu mām । avatu vaktāram avatu vaktāram ॥ oṃ śāntiḥ śāntiḥ śāntiḥ ॥

## Peace Invocation

O Lord!

In my speech, may my awareness be fully present. May I be conscious of my tongue at all times.

Lord please give me your precious time, may I affirm those divine moments when I am at total rest.

May the sacred texts beckon to me and speak to me. May I truly recall, recollect, and apply the wisdom.

May I follow the protocols of society. May I be true to my heart and convictions.

May you protect me and my master, my school and my employer. May my family and environs be safe.

May the one who guides me be fully blessed.
Peace in our heart, in our body and in our environs.

अथ ऐतरेय–उपनिषद् (ऐतरेयोपनिषद्)
atha Aitareya Upaniṣad

## Now begins ऐAiतtaरेreयya Aitareya

Vowel Sandhi – Guna Sandhi – अ + उ → ओ
ऐतरेय + उपनिषद् →ऐतरेयोपनिषद् ।

Note – This is an internal Sandhi, since ऐतरेयोपनिषद् is a compound word.

---

## Cast of Characters

BRAHMAN
VIRAT *or* MAYA
DIVINE ADMINISTRATORS

The discourse giver = Aitareya Rishi
The listener = Devotee = you or me.

## None Other

In the forgotten past, in the far unseen beginnings, there was only the lone आत्मा Atman, the Soul. A thought sprang up seemingly in the Atman, a wish for diversity.

## Origin – the Thought

That thoughtful wish gave rise to infinite planes, planes with distinct natural laws, some intersecting, others entirely unrelated.

## Infrastructure – the 4 Planes

For our current study, we enumerate four planes

- अम्भस् **ambh**, the plane of dark matter.
- मरीची **marīchī**, the plane of light energy.
- मर **mar**, the plane of cyclic duality.
- अप् **ap**, the plane of hidden currents.

## Energy – the Virāt

Then the story goes, another thoughtful wish arose. A desire to have administration. This manifested as विराट् Virāt, a massive column of energy.

## Administration – the Deities

From the massive energy column burst forth various deities and their associated paraphernalia to govern the infrastructure. Each Deity consisted of

- इन्द्रिय Indriya, the sensing apparatus.
- इन्द्रियगोलक Indriyagolak, the housing spaces for the senses.
- इन्द्रिय–अधिष्ठाता Indriya-Adhiṣṭhātā, the chief deity for each sense.

## Birth – the Biology

All births were given a threefold आवस्थ Staging.

- Love making.
- Pregnancy.
- Birth.

- Womb embryo.
- Walking talking body.
- Genetic lineage that continued.

- Waking State.
- Dreaming State.
- Deep Sleep State.

## Need – the Want

As a natural consequence, each deity got infused with the need to fulfill itself. It took the shape of a triple longing

- Food.
- Work and Companionship.
- Pleasure and Entertainment.

## Fulfillment – the Three

The moment of final reckoning arrived. The needs were richly satiated, using three principles

- गौ Gau, Cow products to satisfy food.
- अश्व Aśva, Horse for work-travel-company.
- मनुष्य Man, for utter unending entertainment.

and in turn arose integration.

## Grasping – How to Eat? How to Digest?

The senses failed to grasp. The mind failed to reason.

### Glue – the Apana Vayu

When the end-to-end chain of components all got fashioned, they could not be fitted together. The senses failed to grasp, the mind failed to reason. Then Glue arose to integrate them all into an independent functioning unit. It was named अपान वायु Apana Vayu, the binding assimilating breath.

and in turn arose responsibility.

### Responsibility – the Balance

Finally the Lord decided to lend a hand.

The responsibility of shouldering the creation fell squarely on his shoulders, but he decided not to do it openly, so as not to miss the fun, that being his prime motive in starting the whole thing.

Very ingeniously, the Lord made

- ब्रह्मरान्द्र Brahmarāndra, invisible orifice in the head, sutures in the skull, for his entry-exit.
- हृदय Heart's deep recesses for his resting place.
- गुरु–शिष्य-परंपरा कृपा च Guru Śiṣya parampara and Grace as the means to uniting with him.

## Awakening – the Indra

Consciousness or Soul has been denoted by the varied components within every being

- हृदय Heart, the heart filled with love
- मनस् Mind, the mind of cheerful innocence
- संज्ञानं Knowledge that is unbiased
- आज्ञानं Order and Discipline
- विज्ञानं Science
- प्रज्ञानं Consciousness
- मेधा Intelligence
- दृष्टिः Vision and Mission
- धृतिः Endurance
- मतिः Firm opinion
- मनीषा Free will
- जूति Shyness and coyness
- स्मृतिः Memory power
- संकल्पः Determination
- क्रतु High ideal
- काम Intense passion
- वश Sense of strong ownership

Consciousness is in fact every imaginable and unforeseen name and form. Each and everything

- living and non-living;
- animal, tree, human and alien;
- sand, grain, television and vehicle

is the reflection of the Supreme Consciousness.

The entire visible and invisible spectrum is

- Established in the Supreme Consciousness
- InspiredNourished by SupremeConsciousness
- Willed by the Supreme Consciousness

Consciousness is

- Beyond right and wrong
- Beyond logic and senses
- Everything and Nothing simultaneously

Consciousness has been equated to (only for teaching)

- The Sun as all-pervading light
- The Space as the container of all and as unaffected by anything
- The Pure White screen on which a movie is projected

The One who assimilates this knowledge and lives this wisdom

- shakes off all shackles,
- exits from guilt and grief,
- gets firmly established in Advaita,
- ceases to hanker for cravings,
- attains union with the Divine, and
- is known as the Eternally Blissful.

# 1st Chapter 1st Section

## लीला Leela = the Divine Will

ॐ

आत्मा वा इदमेक एवाग्र आसीन्नान्यत्किञ्चन मिषत् ।

स ईक्षत लोकान्नु सृजा इति ॥ १.१.१

oṃ

ātmā vā idameka evāgra āsīn nānyat kiñcana miṣat |

sa īkṣata lokān nu sṛjā iti || 1.1.1

<u>पदच्छेदः</u>

आत्मा[m1/1] वै[0] इदम्[n1/1] एकः[m1/1] एव[0] अग्रे[n7/1] आसीत्[iii/1 लङ्] न[0]
अन्यत्[0] किञ्चन[0] मिषत्[PrPA शतृ n1/1] ।
सः[m1/1] ईक्षत[iii/1 लङ्] लोकान्[m2/3] नु[0] सृजै[i/1 लोट्] इति[0] ॥

<u>अन्वयः</u>

अग्रे वै in the timeless beginnings इदम् this एकः one आत्मा soul एव alone आसीत् । was there. किञ्चन any अन्यत् other न not मिषत् । is ogling. सः नु and he "लोकान् the worlds सृजानि let me create" इति thus ऐक्षत ॥ thought.

---

आत्मा from आत्मान् from Root 38 अत सातत्यगमने । मिषत् from Root 1352 मिष स्पर्धायाम् । सृजै इति by ayava and then elision sandhi is सृजा इति । सृजै from Root 1414 सृज विसर्गे । This Root is parasmaipadi सृजानि however Vedic usage is atmanepadi सृजै । ईक्षत is Vedic usage for ऐक्षत from Root 610 ईक्ष दर्शने ।

**1.1.1** Before the beginning only the one Soul existed. There was naught else. The Soul willed – "**Let me create Planes of Play**". In Sanskrit the term is लीला Leela = the Divine Play.

Origin or Big Bang has been visualized by the ancient Seers as a 3-step matrix, with an underlying 4th facet.

1. Consciousness a perfect Stillness.
2. Consciousness projects a single Entity, its power known as Virat or Maya.
3. Conscious Projection differentiates into infinite planes, worlds, universes, intelligences, elements, energies, timeframes.

This matrix has the underlying facet that the Consciousness and its Conscious Projection display a sinusoidal character,

- exhibiting, dissolving – manifest, unmanifest. This facet is reflected as the duality in creation in all aspects.

It is known as the first law to be taught, studied, ingrained and learnt; to lead a happy life.

**Opposite Values are Complementary in Nature**
**Sri Sri Ravi Shankar**

Some things may be perceived as ugly, cruel, or disdainful. No matter, do not stain your heart, act from the intellect as per the norms of society, do not become bitter.

स इमाँल्लोकान् असृजत । अम्भो मरीचीर्मरमापोऽदोऽम्भः परेण दिवं द्यौः प्रतिष्ठाऽन्तरिक्षं मरीचयः पृथिवी मरो या अधस्तात्ता आपः ॥ १.१.२

sa imām̐llokān asṛjata । ambho marīcīrmaramāpo'do'mbhaḥ pareṇa divaṃ dyauḥ pratiṣṭhā'ntarikṣaṃ marīcayaḥ pṛthivī maro yā adhastāttā āpaḥ ॥ 1.1.2

सः m1/1 इमान् m2/3 लोकान् m2/3 असृजत iii/1 लङ् । अम्भः n2/1 मरीचीः f2/3 मरम् m2/1 आपः f1/3 अदः n1/1 अम्भः n2/1 परेण 0 दिवं f2/1 द्यौः f1/1 प्रतिष्ठा f1/1 अन्तरिक्षं n1/1 मरीचयः f1/3 पृथिवी f1/1 मरः m1/1 या f1/1 अधस्तात् 0 ताः f1/3 आपः f1/3 ॥

सः he इमान् these लोकान् worlds असृजत । created.
(namely) अम्भः celestial flowing plane, मरीचीः luminous planes, मरम् cyclic plane (and) आपः underground waters.
अदः that
परेण farthest दिवं celestial अम्भः vaporous fluidic plane द्यौः प्रतिष्ठा with sky as support, अन्तरिक्षं interstellar मरीचयः galactic planes, पृथिवी solar system मरः cyclic plane, अधस्तात् nearest या than ताः all those आपः ॥

---

असृजत = असृजत् from Root 1414 सृज विसर्गे । This Root is parasmaipadi असृजत् however Vedic usage is atmanepadi असृजत ।

### 1.1.2 Planes of Existence

By the soul's willing, many diverse planes of existence sprouted. The Principal four planes are mentioned to account for infinity.

- अम्भस् Dark Matter and Energy = Black Hole
- मरीची Stellar Dust & Galaxies=Star Systems
- मर Cyclical = Planetary Systems
- अप् Subterranean Waters=Hidden Emotion

Notice that

- अम्भस् is neuter-neutral by definition
- मरीची is feminine by definition
- मर is masculine by definition
- अप् again feminine since that gives birth

Diverse meaning separated and distinct in terms of natural laws, governing principles, life forms, modes of intelligence, concepts of right and wrong, definitions of essential and redundant.

---

इमान् from इदम् । अम्भः from अम्भस् । मरीचीः from मरीची । अदः from अदस् । ताः from तद् ।

स ईक्षतेमे नु लोका लोकपालान् नु सृजा इति । सोऽद्भ्य एव पुरुषं समुद्धृत्यामूर्च्छयत् ॥ १.१.३

sa īkṣateme nu lokā lokapālān nu sṛjā iti । so'dbhya eva puruṣaṃ samuddhṛtyāmūrcchayat ॥ 1.1.3

सः [m1/1] ईक्षत [iii/1 लङ्] इमे [m1/3] नु [0] लोकाः [m1/3] लोकपालान् [m1/3] नु [0] सृजै [i/1 लोट्] इति [0] । सः [m1/1] अद्भ्यः [f5/3] एव [0] पुरुषं [m2/1] समुद्धृत्य [0 gerund ल्यप्] अमूर्च्छयत् [iii/1 लङ्] ॥

सः he नु then ईक्षत contemplated "(for) इमे these लोकाः worlds लोकपालान् administrators नु verily सृजै let me create" इति । thus.

सः he अद्भ्यः from the waters एव as if समुद्धृत्य having popped up पुरुषं a figure अमूर्च्छयत् ॥ fashioned.

---

अद्भ्यः from अप् । सृजै from Root 1414 सृज विसर्गे । This Root is parasmaipadi सृजानि however Vedic usage is atmanepadi सृजै । ईक्षत is Vedic usage for ऐक्षत from Root 610 ईक्ष दर्शने ।

### 1.1.3 Law and Governance

Typical planes are
अम्भः plane of dark viscous fluids and gluey wetness,
मरीचीः plane of lights and brilliant intellect.
मरम् plane of cyclical adventures,
आपः plane of hidden waters and their denizens.

To house these planes and make them functional and their laws non-intersecting, the space was seemingly divided into

- black matter or black holes with no identifiable phenomena
- galactic matter with luminous bodies and measurable activity
- solar systems with cyclic seasons, cyclic habitation, cyclic birth.
- worlds which preferred to be hidden, mysterious phenomena that couldn't be explained, couldn't be relied upon, couldn't be replicated.

Then the Divine willed Governance, and it took the shape of a massive human body. The "human body" is just an after thought. We can more accurately say a huge figure that covered the entire space housing the three मरीची, मर and अप् planes. The rest of this Upanishad leaves out the अम्भस् plane of dark matter.

तमभ्यतपत्तस्याभितप्तस्य मुखं निरभिद्यत यथाऽण्डं मुखाद्
वाग्वाचोऽग्निर्नासिके निरभिद्येतां नासिकाभ्यां प्राणः ।
प्राणाद् वायुरक्षिणी निरभिद्येतामक्षिभ्यां चक्षुश्चक्षुष आदित्यः कर्णौ
निरभिद्येतां कर्णाभ्यां श्रोत्रं श्रोत्राद्दिशस्त्वङ् निरभिद्यत त्वचो लोमानि
लोमभ्य ओषधिवनस्पतयो हृदयं निरभिद्यत हृदयान्मनो मनसश्चन्द्रमा
नाभिर्निरभिद्यत नाभ्या अपानोऽपानान्मृत्युः शिश्नं निरभिद्यत
शिश्नाद्रेतो रेतस आपः ॥ १.१.४

tamabhyatapattasyābhitaptasya mukhaṃ nirabhidyata
yathā'ṇḍaṃ mukhād vāgvāco'gnirnāsike nirabhidyetāṃ
nāsikābhyāṃ prāṇaḥ I prāṇād vāyurakṣiṇī
nirabhidyetāmakṣibhyāṃ cakṣuścakṣuṣa ādityaḥ karṇau
nirabhidyetāṃ karṇābhyāṃ śrotraṃ śrotrāddiśastvaṅ
nirabhidyata tvaco lomāni lomabhya oṣadhivanaspatayo
hṛdayaṃ nirabhidyata hṛdayānmano manasaścandramā
nābhirnirabhidyata nābhyā apāno'pānānmṛtyuḥ śiśnaṃ
nirabhidyata śiśnādreto retasa āpaḥ II 1.1.4

तम्[m1/1] अभ्यतपत्[iii/1 लङ्] तस्य[m6/1] अभितप्तस्य[PPP m6/1] मुखं[n1/1] निरभिद्यत[iii/1 लङ्] यथा[0] अण्डं[n1/1] मुखात्[n5/1] वाक्[f1/1] वाचः[f5/1] अग्निः[m1/1] नासिके[f1/2] निरभिद्येतां[iii/2 लङ्] नासिकाभ्यां[f5/2] प्राणः[m1/1]।
प्राणात्[m5/1] वायुः[m1/1] अक्षिणी[n1/2] निरभिद्येताम्[iii/2 लङ्] अक्षिभ्यां[n5/2] चक्षुः[n1/1] चक्षुषः[n5/1] आदित्यः[m1/1] कर्णौ[m1/2] निरभिद्येतां[iii/2 लङ्] कर्णाभ्यां[m5/2] श्रोत्रं[n1/1] श्रोत्रात्[n5/1] दिशः[f1/3] त्वक्[f1/1] निरभिद्यत[iii/1 लङ्] त्वचः[f5/1] लोमानि[n1/3] लोमभ्यः[n5/3] ओषधि–वनस्पतयः[m1/3] हृदयं[n1/1] निरभिद्यत[iii/1 लङ्] हृदयात्[n5/1] मनः[n1/1] मनसः[n5/1] चन्द्रमाः[n1/1] नाभिः[f1/1] निरभिद्यत[iii/1 लङ्] नाभ्याः[f5/1] अपानः[m1/1] अपानात्[m5/1] मृत्युः[m1/1] शिश्नं[n1/1] निरभिद्यत[iii/1 लङ्] शिश्नात्[n5/1] रेतः[n1/1] रेतसः[n5/1] आपः[f1/3] ॥

## 1.1.4 Deities for Administration.

Now that infrastructure is done, let me make principles for rulership and efficient governance.

Lo and Behold, subConsciousness or the power of Brahman was thus born. It gave rise to
**mouth** that gave rise to expression that gave rise to heat. The expression became modulated as speech, while heat got the body of fire.
**nose** that gave rise to sensing that gave rise to the life force that gave rise to air. Sensing became modulated as smell and intuition. The **life force** became the unit of life and air became the mechanism of carrying the life force.
**eyes** that gave rise to sight that gave rise to the light. Sight became modulated as vision and clear thought, and light got housed in the body of the Sun.
**ears** that gave rise to sound that expanded as space.
**skin** that gave rise to fine strands that gave rise to grass, herb, tree.
**heart** that created the mind that gave rise to waxing and waning. The mind housed thoughts and emotions which were always in a flux, thereby the moon was fashioned to substantiate the mind's modulations.
**navel** that gave rise to a gut that was prone to aging and dissolution.
**genitals** that gave birth to new seed that needed fertile fluids to propagate. The fertile fluids got housed in a body of water.

तम् He the massive figure अभ्यतपत् deeply meditated. तस्य अभितप्तस्य Of his deep penance मुखं a face निरभिद्यत popped up यथा just like अण्डं a fertilized egg.

मुखात् From the face

वाक् Speech, वाचः from speech अग्निः heat.

नासिके Two nostrils निरभिद्येतां popped out, नासिकाभ्यां from nostrils प्राणः life breath, प्राणात् from life breath वायुः the Air.

अक्षिणी Two eyes निरभिद्येताम् popped out अक्षिभ्यां from eyes चक्षुः vision चक्षुषः from vision आदित्यः the Sun.

कर्णौ Two ears निरभिद्येतां popped out, कर्णाभ्यां from ears श्रोत्रं hearing, श्रोत्रात् from hearing दिशः the four corners.

त्वक् Skin निरभिद्यत mushroomed, त्वचः from skin लोमानि hair, लोमभ्यः from hair ओषधि–वनस्पतयः herbs and vegetables.

हृदयं Heart निरभिद्यत opened up, हृदयात् from heart मनः mind मनसः from mind चन्द्रमाः the moon.

नाभिः Solar Plexus निरभिद्यत popped, नाभ्याः from navel अपानः Digestive Breath अपानात् from Apana Vayu मृत्युः the Exit.

शिश्नं phallus निरभिद्यत shot up, शिश्नात् from phallus रेतः the seed रेतसः from seed आपः ॥ waters and fluids.

---

चन्द्रमाः m1/1 from चन्द्रमस् ।

The 3 aspects of Brahman

We have seen the three aspects of Brahman as

- Unqualified undifferentiated Brahman
- Maya = a Power of Brahman
- Principal Features of Maya viz. Senses, AntahKarana, Digestion & Exit

# Qualifications for an aspirant

Traditionally, each seeker is advised to perfect these traits so that the Upanishad can be properly श्रवणं understood, मननं practiced, and निधिध्यासनं assimilated.

साधन–चतुष्टय the 4 personality traits:

1) Trusting, discriminating attitude. विवेकः Viveka.

2) Dispassion or restraint in matters unconnected to job. Not overstepping one's domain. वैराग्यं Vairagya.

3) Willingness and endurance to persevere for a length of time, e.g. a year. षट् सम्पत्तिः Shat Sampatti.

4) A desire to learn, evolve, become more useful. मुमुक्षुत्वं Mumukshutva.

# 1st Chapter 2nd Section

## लीला Leela = Divine's Subtle Domain

ता एता देवताः सृष्टा अस्मिन् महत्यर्णवे प्रापतंस्तमशनाया-पिपासाभ्यामन्ववार्जत् । ता एनमब्रुवन्नायतनं नः प्रजानीहि यस्मिन् प्रतिष्ठिता अन्नमदामेति ॥ १.२.१

tā etā devatāḥ sṛṣṭā asmin mahatyarṇave prāpataṃstamaśanāyā-pipāsābhyāmanvavārjat । tā enamabruvannāyatanaṃ naḥ prajānīhi yasmin pratiṣṭhitā annamadāmeti ॥ 1.2.1

ताः [f1/3] एताः [f1/3] देवताः [f1/3] सृष्टाः [PPP f1/3] अस्मिन् [m7/1] महति [m7/1] अर्णवे [m7/1] प्रापतन् [iii/3 लङ्] तम् [m2/1] अशनाया-पिपासाभ्याम् [f3/2] अन्ववार्जत् [iii/1 लङ्] । ताः [f1/3] एनम् [m2/1] अब्रुवन् [iii/3 लङ्] आयतनं [n2/1] नः [f4/3] प्रजानीहि [ii/1 लोट्] यस्मिन् [n7/1] प्रतिष्ठिताः [PPP n1/3] अन्नम् [n1/1] अदाम [i/3 लोट्] इति [0] ॥

ताः those referred to earlier, एताः these सृष्टाः manifested देवताः divine administrators अस्मिन् in this महति great अर्णवे ocean प्रापतन् spreading out fell. तम् he the Virat figure अशनाया-पिपासाभ्याम् with hunger and thirst अन्ववार्जत् । was infused. ताः they एनम् to the Brahman अब्रुवन् pleaded " नः for us आयतनं space प्रजानीहि please indicate यस्मिन् wherein प्रतिष्ठिताः being well established अन्नम् nourishment अदाम we may get", इति ॥ thus.

### 1.2.1 Nourishment

Now that the infrastructure and the governing principles having been fashioned, a strong need was felt to feast, enjoy and entertain.

For the Divine Leela to proceed, a mechanism was willed by Brahman. This mechanism is known as need for

- Food
- Company
- Pleasure

---

प्रापतन् from प्र+आ+Root 845 पत्ऌ गतौ । अन्ववार्जत् from अनु+अव+Root 224 अर्ज अर्जने । अदाम from Root 1011 अद भक्षणे । प्रजानीहि from प्र+Root 1507 ज्ञा अवबोधने ।

ताभ्यो गामानयत्ता अब्रुवन्न वै नोऽयमलमिति ।
ताभ्योऽश्वमानयत्ता अब्रुवन्न वै नोऽयमलमिति ॥ १.२.२

tābhyo gāmānayattā abruvanna vai no'yamalamiti |
tābhyo'śvamānayattā abruvanna vai no'yamalamiti || 1.2.2

ताभ्यः $^{f4/3}$ गाम् $^{f2/1}$ आनयत् $^{iii/1}$लङ् ताः $^{f1/3}$ अब्रुवन् $^{iii/3}$लङ् न $^{0}$ वै $^{0}$ नः $^{f2/3}$ अयम् $^{m1/1}$ अलम् $^{0}$ इति $^{o}$ ।
ताभ्यः $^{f4/3}$ अश्वम् $^{m2/1}$ आनयत् $^{iii/1}$लङ् ताः $^{f1/3}$ अब्रुवन् $^{iii/3}$लङ् न $^{0}$ वै $^{0}$ नः $^{f2/3}$ अयम् $^{m1/1}$ अलम् $^{0}$ इति $^{o}$ ।

ताभ्यः for the divinities गाम् figure of a cow आनयत् was displayed. ताः they अब्रुवन् responded “अयम् this वै certainly नः for us न is not अलम् sufficient”, इति । thus. ताभ्यः for them अश्वम् figure of a horse आनयत् was brought. ताः they अब्रुवन् reacted “अयम् this वै certainly नः for us न is not अलम् good enough”, इति । thus.

### 1.2.2 Cow, Horse

This Need took the form of a devotee and prayed. The prayer was answered in stages. The first need of hunger was satisfied by the manifestation of the Cow, source of milk and all delicious sweetmeats.

The adjunct need of social company was fulfilled by the manifestation of the Horse, source of speedy travel to distant lands, and an understanding companion to boot.

Finally the desire for entertainment was also satiated, by the superb construction of a human being. With its thoroughly unpredictable nature, huge craving for pleasure and comfort, vast ingenuity and adaptability, a human being became the perfect toy for the creator's undiluted entertainment.

**Cow Horse Human = Food Company Pleasure**

So we see, a cow is the principal source of all food items. Cow represents Milk = mother's milk and Ghee or clarified butter and Cowdung the farm fertilizer.

A horse is the perfect companion. It represents society for work and cultural activity and a partner for close comradeship.

Human Being is here alluded to as a pleasure giving element.

ताभ्यः पुरुषमानयत्ता अब्रुवन् सुकृतं बतेति । पुरुषो वाव सुकृतम् ।
ता अब्रवीद्यथायतनं प्रविशतेति ॥ १.२.३

tābhyaḥ puruṣamānayattā abruvan sukṛtaṃ bateti ।
puruṣo vāva sukṛtam । tā abravīdyathāyatanaṃ praviśateti
॥ 1.2.3

ताभ्यः [f4/3] पुरुषम् [m2/1] आनयत् [iii/1 लङ्] ताः [f1/3] अब्रुवन् [iii/3 लङ्] सुकृतं [PPP m2/1] बत[0] इति[0] ।
पुरुषः [m1/1] वाव[0] सुकृतम् [PPP m2/1] । ताः [f1/3] अब्रवीत् [iii/1 लङ्] यथा-आयतनं [0] प्रविशत [ii/3 लोट्] इति [0] ॥

ताभ्यः for the deities पुरुषम् the figure of a human being आनयत् was fetched. ताः they अब्रुवन् exulted, "सुकृतं beautifully done बत excellent!", इति । thus.
पुरुषः the human form वाव truly सुकृतम् । is magnificently done.
ताः to the administrators अब्रवीत् he said, "यथा-आयतनं each your respective place प्रविशत you may take", इति ॥ thus.

---

वाव = वै एव । Used as a compound word also.
प्रविशत from प्र+Root 845 विश प्रवेशने ।

### 1.2.3 Human and the Placements

Correct Placement and Seating as per ability ensures holistic growth and proper nourishment.

Now all the natural forces took their respective places in the body of a being. The deity of sight, the deity of sound, and the other Shaktis got themselves established.

Once the role of an individual is clearly allocated, he can start performance of duty to his optimal capacity. Responsibility whether at work or at home can be fully shouldered when the framework is well-defined and the role is cleanly allocated.

अग्निर्वाग्भूत्वा मुखं प्राविशद् वायुः प्राणो भूत्वा नासिके
प्राविशदादित्यश्चक्षुर्भूत्वा अक्षिणी प्राविशद्दिशः श्रोत्रं भूत्वा कर्णौ
प्राविशन्नोषधिवनस्पतयो लोमानि भूत्वा त्वचं प्राविशंश्चन्द्रमा मनो भूत्वा हृदयं
प्राविशन्मृत्युरपानो भूत्वा नाभिं प्राविशदापो रेतो भूत्वा शिश्नं प्राविशन् ॥
agnirvāgbhūtvā mukhaṃ prāviśad vāyuḥ prāṇo bhūtvā
nāsike prāviśadādityaścakṣurbhūtvā akṣiṇī prāviśaddiśaḥ
śrotraṃ bhūtvā karṇau prāviśannoṣadhivanaspatayo
lomāni bhūtvā tvacaṃ prāviśaṃścandramā mano bhūtvā
hṛdayaṃ prāviśanmṛtyurapāno bhūtvā nābhiṃ prāviśadāpo
reto bhūtvā śiśnaṃ prāviśan || 1.2.4

अग्निः [m1/1] वाक् [f1/1] भूत्वा [0] मुखं [n2/1] प्राविशत् [iii/1 लङ्] वायुः [m1/1] प्राणः [m1/1] भूत्वा [0] नासिके [f2/2] प्राविशत् [iii/1 लङ्] आदित्यः [m1/1] चक्षुः [n1/1] भूत्वा [0] अक्षिणी [n2/2] प्राविशत् [iii/1 लङ्] दिशः [f1/3] श्रोत्रं [n1/1] भूत्वा [f1/3] कर्णौ [m2/2] प्राविशत् [iii/1 लङ्] ओषधि–वनस्पतयः [m1/3] लोमानि [n1/3] भूत्वा [0] त्वचं [f2/1] प्राविशत् [iii/1 लङ्] चन्द्रमाः [m1/1] मनः [n1/1] भूत्वा [0] हृदयं [n2/1] प्राविशत् [iii/1 लङ्] मृत्युः [m1/1] अपानः [m1/1] भूत्वा [0] नाभिं [f2/1] प्राविशत् [iii/1 लङ्] आपः [f1/3] रेतः [n1/1] भूत्वा [0] शिश्नं [n2/1] प्राविशन् [iii/3 लङ्] ॥

अग्निः The divinity Heat वाक् speech भूत्वा having become मुखं the mouth प्राविशत् got stationed. वायुः The deity Air प्राणः prana भूत्वा having made नासिके both nostrils प्राविशत् activated. आदित्यः The Sun चक्षुः eye भूत्वा having made अक्षिणी the eyes प्राविशत् energized. दिशः the four Quarters श्रोत्रं hearing भूत्वा having become कर्णौ two ears प्राविशत् impregnated. ओषधि–वनस्पतयः the herbs and vegetables लोमानि hair भूत्वा having become त्वचं skin प्राविशत् made. चन्द्रमाः the Moon मनः mind भूत्वा having made हृदयं heart प्राविशत् entered. मृत्युः Final Exit अपानः Apana vayu भूत्वा having become नाभिं Navel Center प्राविशत् irradiated. आपः the waters रेतः seed भूत्वा having fashioned शिश्नं the linga प्राविशन् ॥ moved into.

## 1.2.4 The functional Matrix

An outline of the geometry and anatomy of the Deities functioning within an individual is stated.

| Lord of governing Deity | | Purpose | Anatomy |
|---|---|---|---|
| Agni | Heat | Speech = Expression | Mouth |
| Vayu | Air | Breath = Life | Nostrils |
| Aditya | Light | Vision = Plan, Aim | Eyes |
| Disha | Space | Hearing = Coordinates, Limits, Alertness | Ears |
| Aushadhi | Flora | Hair = Universality, Nourishment, Appearance | Skin |
| Chandra | Mind | Antahkarna = Thought, Emotion, Bank Balance | Heart |
| Mrityu | Exit | Apana Vayu = Digestion | Navel |
| Aapaḥ | Seed | Procreation = Joy, Continuity | Phallus |

---

चन्द्रमाः from चन्द्रमस् । प्राविशत् iii/1 लङ् । प्राविशन् iii/3 लङ् । आपः from अप् । Always declines in plural.

तमशनायापिपासे अब्रूतामावाभ्याममभिप्रजानीहीति । ते अब्रवीदेतास्वेव वां देवतास्वाभजाम्येतासु भागिन्यौ करोमीति । तस्माद् यस्यै कस्यै च देवतायै हविर्गृह्यते भागिन्यावेवास्यामशनायापिपासे भवतः ॥ १.२.५

tamaśanāyāpipāse abrūtāmāvābhyāmabhiprajānīhīti । te abravīdetāsveva vāṃ devatāsvābhajāmyetāsu bhāginyau karomīti । tasmād yasyai kasyai ca devatāyai havirgṛhyate bhāginyāvevāsyāmaśanāyāpipāse bhavataḥ ॥ 1.2.5

तम्[m2/1] अशनाया–पिपासे[f1/2] अब्रूताम्[iii/2 लङ्] आवाभ्याम्[f3/2] अभिप्रजानीहि[ii/1 लोट्] इति[0] । ते[f2/2] अब्रवीत्[iii/1 लङ्] एतासु[f7/3] एव[0] वां[f2/2] देवतासु[f7/3] आभजामि[i/1 लट्] एतासु[f7/3] भागिन्यौ[f2/2] करोमि[i/1 लट्] इति[0] । तस्मात्[0] यस्यै[f4/1] कस्यै[f4/1] च[0] देवतायै[f4/1] हविः[n1/1] गृह्यते[iii/1 लट् कर्मणि] भागिन्यौ[f2/2] एव[0] अस्याम्[f7/1] अशनाया–पिपासे[f1/2] भवतः[iii/2 लट्] ॥

अशनाया–पिपासे the pair of greed and sadness तम् to Brahman अब्रूताम् queried, "आवाभ्याम् for us both अभिप्रजानीहि kindly specify a dwelling place", इति ।
ते to that pair अब्रवीत् he replied, "वां to you both एतासु amongst all these देवतासु deities एव justly आभजामि। equitably divide, एतासु in all of them भागिन्यौ proportionate sharing for two करोमि I make", इति । *(this statement is repeated to indicate to the discerning that both good-& bad have shortcomings, both likes & dislikes need to be shed on the path).*
तस्मात् hence यस्यै कस्यै च देवतायै for whichever virtue हविः respect and effort गृह्यते is offered, भागिन्यौ एव अस्याम् a portion duly of that respect and effort अशनाया–पिपासे hunger and sadness भवतः ॥ is.

### 1.2.5 Greed and Sadness = Need and Longing

No play is complete without opposing tendencies. These forces keep the fun and uncertainty alive and the play going for long.

The deities of Hunger and Thirst also begged to be accommodated. These forces asked the great Lord regarding the mechanism for their manifestation and support.

To their plea the kind Lord asserted - may you take your lodging and boarding in human beings only, and particularly those that fail to be disciplined, have scant regard for others' welfare, and are apt to skip contributing to the state coffers.

The Upanishad hints at all inclusiveness of the human personality.

# 1st Chapter 3rd Section

## लीला Leela = the Divine loves Anonymity

स ईक्षतेमे नु लोकाश्च लोकपालाश्चान्नमेभ्यः सृजा इति ॥ १.३.१

sa īkṣateme nu lokāśca lokapālāścānnamebhyaḥ sṛjā iti ||
1.3.1

सः ईक्षत He thought,
इमे नु लोकाः च "now these worlds
लोकपालाः च and the governors
अन्नम् एभ्यः modes of sustenance for them
सृजै इति ॥ let me manifest".

1.3.1 A Design that takes care of everything is called holistic design.

In each product or gadget, the design and planning must follow the principles enumerated herein.

Now the Supreme Divinity willed the ultimate product for the Leela – **to keep the Act in continuous Play.**

The final product = FOOD, NEED, WANT, DESIRE.

सोऽपोऽभ्यतपत् ताभ्योऽभितप्ताभ्यो मूर्तिरजायत ।
या वै सा मूर्तिरजायतान्नं वै तत् ॥ १.३.२

so'po'bhyatapat tābhyo'bhitaptābhyo mūrtirajāyata I
yā vai sā mūrtirajāyatānnaṃ vai tat II 1.3.2

सः अपः अभि–अतपत् He waters willed by meditation,
ताभ्यः thereupon waters appeared, and
अभितप्ताभ्यः from those waters willed by meditation
मूर्तिः अजायत । a physical form took shape.

या वै सा मूर्तिः अजायत Indeed the form that so materialized,
अन्नं वै तत् ॥ food wondrously it was.

---

अपः f2/3 from अप् । Always declines in plural.

1.3.2 Lots of meditative thinking, paperwork, scratch pad, thinktank, is what aids research and development.

Without serious thought, integrity of product cannot be established. Without proper aesthetics even the best design falls short.

“Waters” signify the fluid framework for

- love to blossom,
- emotions to be nurtured,
- thought to manifest.

After the framework is ready, a concrete form can materialize.

तदेनत्सृष्टं पराङत्यजिघांसत् । तद् वाचाऽजिघृक्षत् तन्नाशक्नोद्वाचा ग्रहीतुम् । स यद्धैनद्वाचाऽग्रहैष्यदभिव्याहृत्य हैवान्नमत्रप्स्यत् ॥ १.३.३

tadenatsṛṣṭaṃ parāṅatyajighāṃsat I tad vācā'jighṛkṣat tannāśaknodvācā grahītum I sa yaddhainadvācā'grahaiṣyadabhivyāhṛtya haivānnamatrapsyat II 1.3.3

तत् n1/1 एनत् n2/1 सृष्टं PPP n1/1 पराक् 0 अति–अजिघांसत् iii/1 सन् लङ् । तत् n1/1 वाचा m3/1 अजिघृक्षत् iii/1 सन् लङ् तत् n1/1 न 0 अशक्नोत् iii/1 लङ् वाचा m3/1 ग्रहीतुम् infinitive । सः m1/1 यत् n1/1 ह 0 एनत् n2/1 वाचा m3/1 अग्रहैष्यत् iii/1 लृङ् अभिव्याहृत्य gerund ह 0 एव 0 अन्नम् n2/1 अत्रप्स्यत् iii/1 सन् लङ् ॥

तत् from that Virat figure wishing for food, एनत् this सृष्टं created food पराक् turning away अति–अजिघांसत् । speedily-wished to flee.

वाचा by speech तत् that food अजिघृक्षत् was wished to be partaken of, वाचा however only the speech तत् that food ग्रहीतुम् to grasp न अशक्नोत् । was not competent enough.
यत् ह Because एनत् this food, सः he the Virat वाचा by expression अग्रहैष्यत् if could grasp,
अभिव्याहृत्य ह एव just an expressive speech अन्नम् nourishment अत्रप्स्यत् ॥ could have satisfied.

1.3.3 Initially there is the stage of beta testing before any product launch.

By word of mouth developers are initially contacted. However word of mouth is not enough.

For a meeting and a plan, initially a call goes through, however just a phone call will never make it a success.

Needs are not completely satisfied by Speech.

तत् प्राणेनाजिघृक्षत् तन्नाशक्नोत् प्राणेन ग्रहीतुम् ।
स यद्धैनत्प्राणेनाग्रहैष्यदभिप्राण्य हैवान्नमत्रप्स्यत् ॥ १.३.४

tat prāṇenājighṛkṣat tannāśaknot prāṇena grahītum |
sa yaddhainatprāṇenāgrahaiṣyadabhiprāṇya
haivānnamatrapsyat || 1.3.4

तत्[n1/1] प्राणेन[m3/1] अजिघृक्षत्[iii/1 सन् लङ्] तत्[n1/1] न[0] अशक्नोत्[iii/1 लङ्] प्राणेन[m3/1] ग्रहीतुम्[infinitive] । सः[m1/1] यत्[n1/1] ह[0] एनत्[n2/1] प्राणेन[m3/1] अग्रहैष्यत्[iii/1 लृङ्] अभिप्राण्य[gerund] ह[0] एव[0] अन्नम्[n2/1] अत्रप्स्यत्[iii/1 सन् लङ्] ॥

प्राणेन by breath तत् that food अजिघृक्षत् was wished to be partaken of, प्राणेन however only by the breath तत् that food ग्रहीतुम् to grasp न अशक्नोत् । he was not competent enough.

यत् ह Because एनत् this food, सः he the Virat प्राणेन by breath अग्रहैष्यत् if could grasp,
अभिप्राण्य ह एव just a deep breath अन्नम् nourishment अत्रप्स्यत् ॥ could have satisfied.

1.3.4 And then other methods are added. After an initial phone call, a sense of urgency is infused in the message.

However even that falls short.

Needs are not completely met by Urgency, fast breathing, or deep breath.

तच्चक्षुषाऽजिघृक्षत् तन्नाशक्नोच्चक्षुषा ग्रहीतुम् ।
स यद्धैनच्चक्षुषाऽग्रहैष्यद् दृष्ट्वा हैवान्नमत्रप्स्यत् ॥ १.३.५

tac cakṣuṣā'jighṛkṣat tannāśaknoccakṣuṣā grahītum ।
sa yaddhainaccakṣuṣā'grahaiṣyad dṛṣṭvā
haivānnamatrapsyat ॥ 1.3.5

तत् n1/1 चक्षुषा n3/1 अजिघृक्षत् iii/1 सन् लङ् तत् n1/1 न 0 अशक्नोत् iii/1 लङ् चक्षुषा n3/1 ग्रहीतुम् infinitive । सः m1/1 यत् n1/1 ह 0 एनत् n2/1 चक्षुषा n3/1 अग्रहैष्यत् iii/1 लृङ् दृष्ट्वा gerund ह 0 एव 0 अन्नम् n2/1 अत्रप्स्यत् iii/1 सन् लङ् ॥

चक्षुषा by vision तत् that food अजिघृक्षत् was wished to be partaken of, चक्षुषा however only by the vision तत् that food ग्रहीतुम् to grasp न अशक्नोत् । he was not competent enough.

यत् ह Because एनत् this food, सः he the Virat प्राणेन by vision अग्रहैष्यत् if could grasp,
दृष्ट्वा ह एव just having sharp eyesight अन्नम् nourishment अत्रप्स्यत् ॥ could have satisfied.

1.3.5 Display posters, pamphlets, and eye-catching advertisements are next made and circulated.

Even then success is not guaranteed.

Needs are not fulfilled by Visionary statements.

तच्छ्रोत्रेणाजिघृक्षत् तन्नाशक्नोच्छ्रोत्रेण ग्रहीतुम् ।
स यद्धैनच्छ्रोत्रेणाग्रहैष्यच्छ्रुत्वा हैवान्नमत्रप्स्यत् ॥ १.३.६

tacchrotreṇājighṛkṣat tannāśaknocchrotreṇa grahītum I
sa yaddhainacchrotreṇāgrahaiṣyacchrutvā
haivānnamatrapsyat II 1.3.6

तत्[n1/1] श्रोत्रेण[n3/1] अजिघृक्षत्[iii/1 सन् लङ्] तत्[n1/1] न[0] अशक्नोत्[iii/1 लङ्] श्रोत्रेण[n3/1] ग्रहीतुम्[infinitive] । सः[m1/1] यत्[n1/1] ह[0] एनत्[n2/1] श्रोत्रेण[n3/1] अग्रहैष्यत्[iii/1 लृङ्] श्रुत्वा[gerund] ह[0] एव[0] अन्नम्[n2/1] अत्रप्स्यत्[iii/1 सन् लङ्] ॥

श्रोत्रेण by hearing तत् that food अजिघृक्षत् was wished to be partaken of, श्रोत्रेण however only by the alertness तत् that food ग्रहीतुम् to grasp न अशक्नोत् । he the Virat was not competent enough.

यत् ह Because एनत् this food, सः he the Virat श्रोत्रेण by alertness अग्रहैष्यत् if could grasp,
दृष्ट्वा ह एव just being alert अन्नम् nourishment अत्रप्स्यत् ॥ could have satisfied.

1.3.6 Plays, stage shows, movies, podcasts and radio talk shows are also employed.

We are getting close, but more is necessary.

Needs are not completely satisfied by Alertness and acute listening.

तत् त्वचाऽजिघृक्षत् तन्नाशक्नोत्त्वचा ग्रहीतुम् ।
स यद्धैनत्त्वचाऽग्रहैष्यत् स्पृष्ट्वा हैवान्नमत्रप्स्यत् ॥ १.३.७

tat tvacā'jighṛkṣat tannāśaknottvacā grahītum ।
sa yaddhainattvacā'grahaiṣyat spṛṣṭvā haivānnamatrapsyat
॥ 1.3.7

तत् [n1/1] त्वचा [f3/1] अजिघृक्षत् [iii/1 सन् लङ्] तत् [n1/1] न [0] अशक्नोत् [iii/1 लङ्] त्वचा [f3/1] ग्रहीतुम् [infinitive] । सः [m1/1] यत् [n1/1] ह [0] एनत् [n2/1] त्वचा [f3/1] अग्रहैष्यत् [iii/1 लृङ्] स्पृष्ट्वा [gerund] ह [0] एव [0] अन्नम् [n2/1] अत्रप्स्यत् [iii/1 सन् लङ्] ॥

त्वचा by touch तत् that want अजिघृक्षत् was wished to be seized, त्वचा however only by the close proximity तत् that want ग्रहीतुम् to seize न अशक्नोत् । he the Virat was not competent enough.

यत् ह Because एनत् this want, सः he the Virat त्वचा by close proximity अग्रहैष्यत् if could seize,
स्पृष्ट्वा ह एव just being together अन्नम् want अत्रप्स्यत् ॥
could have satiated.

1.3.7 Close contact is made. Physical touch is employed. Personal visits are arranged.

It is still not enough.

Needs are not completely satisfied by Touch.

तन्मनसाऽजिघृक्षत् तन्नाशक्नोन्मनसा ग्रहीतुम् ।
स यद्धैनन्मनसाऽग्रहैष्यद् ध्यात्वा हैवान्नमत्रप्स्यत् ॥ १.३.८

tanmanasā'jighṛkṣat tannāśaknonmanasā grahītum ।
sa yaddhainanmanasā'grahaiṣyad dhyātvā
haivānnamatrapsyat ॥ 1.3.8

तत् n1/1 मनसा n3/1 अजिघृक्षत् iii/1 सन् लङ् तत् n1/1 न 0 अशक्नोत् iii/1 लङ् मनसा n3/1 ग्रहीतुम् infinitive । सः m1/1 यत् n1/1 ह 0 एनत् n2/1 मनसा n3/1 अग्रहैष्यत् iii/1 लृङ् ध्यात्वा gerund ह 0 एव 0 अन्नम् n2/1 अत्रप्स्यत् iii/1 सन् लङ् ॥

मनसा by intelligence तत् that hunger अजिघृक्षत् was wished to be fulfilled, मनसा however only by the intellect तत् that hunger ग्रहीतुम् to fulfill न अशक्नोत् । he the Virat was not competent enough.

यत् ह Because एनत् this hunger, सः he the Virat मनसा by astute thinking and memory अग्रहैष्यत् if could fulfill,
ध्यात्वा ह एव just thinking and contemplating अन्नम् hunger अत्रप्स्यत् ॥ could have willed and satiated.

1.3.8 Debates are arranged. Discourses are given by renowned orators. Legal attorneys are hired to establish the point.

Still short of the goal.

Needs are not completely satisfied by Intelligence.

तच्छिश्नेनाजिघृक्षत् तन्नाशक्नोच्छिश्नेन ग्रहीतुम् ।
स यद्धैनच्छिश्नेनाग्रहैष्यद् विसृज्य हैवान्नमत्रप्स्यत् ॥ १.३.९

tacchiśnenājighṛkṣat tannāśaknocchiśnena grahītum ।
sa yaddhainacchiśnenāgrahaiṣyad visṛjya
haivānnamatrapsyat ॥ 1.3.9

तत्[n1/1] शिश्नेन[n1/1] अजिघृक्षत्[iii/1 सन् लङ्] तत्[n1/1] न[0] अशक्नोत्[iii/1 लङ्] शिश्नेन[n1/1] ग्रहीतुम्[0 तुमुन्] । सः[m1/1] यत्[n1/1] ह[0] एनत्[n2/1] शिश्नेन[n1/1] अग्रहैष्यत्[iii/1 लृङ्] विसृज्य[0 ल्यप्] ह[0] एव[0] अन्नम्[n2/1] अत्रप्स्यत्[iii/1 सन् लङ्] ॥

शिश्नेन by the phallus तत् that need अजिघृक्षत् was wished to be fulfilled, शिश्नेन however only by intercourse तत् that need ग्रहीतुम् to fulfill न अशक्नोत् । he the Virat was not competent enough.

यत् ह Because एनत् this need, सः he the Virat शिश्नेन by love making अग्रहैष्यत् if could fulfill,
विसृज्य ह एव just dispensing one's seed अन्नम् need अत्रप्स्यत् ॥ could have satiated.

1.3.9 The matter of intimacy is resorted to. Sweetened offers are made. Promises are backed up with juicy perks and privileges.

Something is still amiss.

Needs are not wholly met by Love making.

तदपानेनाजिघृक्षत् तदावयत् ।
सैषोऽन्नस्य ग्रहो यद् वायुरन्नायुर्वा एष यद्वायुः ॥ १.३.१०

tadapānenājighṛkṣat tadāvayat I
saiṣo'nnasya graho yad vāyurannāyurvā eṣa yadvāyuḥ II
1.3.10

तत् n1/1 अपानेन m3/1 अजिघृक्षत् iii/1 सन् लङ् तत् n1/1 आवयत् iii/1 लङ् । सः m1/1 एषः m1/1 अन्नस्य n6/1 ग्रहः m1/1 यत् n1/1 वायुः m1/1 अन्नायुः m1/1 वै 0 एषः m1/1 यत् n1/1 वायुः m1/1 ॥

तत् that desire अपानेन by the Apana vayu अजिघृक्षत् was wished to be assimilated,
तत् that desire आवयत् I got consummated.

एषः अन्नस्य of this food-need-want-desire सः he the Deity Apana Vayu ग्रहः the consumer is,

वायुः the breath यत् which अन्नायुः digests and assimilates food and thought and want,
वै indeed एषः this वायुः force यत् II that is.

---

सः षः by sandhi स एषः । Vedic usage, further vriddhi sandhi, hence सैषः ।

1.3.10 Finally, the method of integration of the complete chain (so far tried in bits and pieces) is employed.

Success.

End-to-end Integration is the key for great success in any venture.

The Apana Vayu or the Digestive Breath is the key to food assimilation and desire fulfillment. It helps to digest thoughts and emotions and knotty issues as well.

Many Yogic methods, Asana, Pranayama and Meditation are advised to maintain a healthy Apana Vayu.

Dharana Dhyana Samadhi helps achieve a very stable Apana Vayu.

स ईक्षत कथं न्विदं मदृते स्यादिति स ईक्षत कतरेण प्रपद्या इति ।
स ईक्षत यदि वाचाऽभिव्याहृतं यदि प्राणेनाभिप्राणितं यदि चक्षुषा दृष्टं यदि श्रोत्रेण श्रुतं यदि त्वचा स्पृष्टं यदि मनसा ध्यातं यद्यपानेनाभ्यपानितं यदि शिश्नेन विसृष्टमथ कोऽहमिति ॥ १.३.११

sa īkṣata kathaṃ nvidaṃ madṛte syāditi sa īkṣata katareṇa prapadyā iti ।
sa īkṣata yadi vācā'bhivyāhṛtaṃ yadi prāṇenābhiprāṇitaṃ yadi cakṣuṣā dṛṣṭaṃ yadi śrotreṇa śrutaṃ yadi tvacā spṛṣṭaṃ yadi manasā dhyātaṃ yadyapānenābhyapānitaṃ yadi śiśnena visṛṣṭamatha ko'hamiti ॥ 1.3.11

सः [m1/1] ईक्षत [iii/1 लङ्] कथं [0] नु [0] इदं [n1/1] मत् [m5/1] ऋते [0] स्यात् [iii/1 विधिलिङ्] इति [0] सः [m1/1] ईक्षत [iii/1 लङ्] कतरेण [m3/1] प्रपद्यै [i/1 लोट्] इति [0] । सः [m1/1] ईक्षत [iii/1 लङ्] यदि [0] वाचा [f3/1] अभिव्याहृतं [PPP n1/1] यदि [0] प्राणेन [m3/1] अभिप्राणितं [PPP n1/1] यदि [0] चक्षुषा [n3/1] दृष्टं [PPP n1/1] यदि [0] श्रोत्रेण [n3/1] श्रुतं [PPP n1/1] यदि [0] त्वचा [f3/1] स्पृष्टं [PPP n1/1] यदि [0] मनसा [n3/1] ध्यातं [PPP n1/1] यदि [0] अपानेन [m3/1] अभि–अपानितं [PPP n1/1] यदि [0] शिश्नेन [n3/1] विसृष्टम् [PPP n1/1] अथ[0] कः [m1/1] अहम् [m1/1] इति [0] ॥

सः he the Brahman ईक्षत reflected "कथं नु now how मत् my bodyMind इदं thing ऋते really स्यात् could function इति । without my conscious presence?"

सः he the Supreme ईक्षत contemplated "कतरेण by what means प्रपद्यै may I enter this?" इति ।

## 1.3.11 The pure exit and reentry is finally planned.

Backwards integration with earlier versions, and keeping in mind future developments and long term viability, the design now incorporates an active reusability mechanism.

The Lord at last figures out that he must fit into the entire scheme of creation, since without his conscious presence it is all just a lifeless mass.

---

सः he the Lord ईक्षत thought

"यदि if वाचा by the Deity Speech alone अभिव्याहृतं expression is possible,
यदि if प्राणेन by the Life force alone अभिप्राणितं life is infused,
यदि if चक्षुषा by the Deity Sight alone दृष्टं vision is possible,
यदि if श्रोत्रेण by the Deity Sound alone श्रुतं hearing,
यदि if त्वचा by the Deity Touch alone स्पृष्टं contact,
यदि if मनसा by the Deity Mind alone ध्यातं thinking,
यदि if अपानेन by the Deity Apana Vayu alone अभि–अपानितं digestion and assimilation and strength,
यदि if शिश्नेन by the Deity Phallus alone विसृष्टम् further creation,

अथ कः अहम् इति ॥ then what could be my role? Then I would be completely redundant isn't it"!

स एतमेव सीमानं विदार्यैतया द्वारा प्रापद्यत । सैषा विद्दतिर्नाम द्वास्तदेतन्नान्दनम् । तस्य त्रय आवसथास्त्रयः स्वप्नाः । अयमावसथोऽयमावसथोऽयमावसथ इति ॥ १.३.१२

sa etameva sīmānaṃ vidāryaitayā dvārā prāpadyata | saiṣā vidṛtirnāma dvāstadetannāndanam | tasya traya āvasathāstrayaḥ svapnāḥ |
ayamāvasatho'yamāvasatho'yamāvasatha iti || 1.3.12

सः m1/1 एतम् m2/1 एव 0 सीमानं m2/1 विदार्य 0 gerund एतया f3/1 द्वारा f3/1 प्रापद्यत iii/1 लङ् । सा f1/1 एषा f1/1 विदृतिः f1/1 नाम 0 द्वाः f1/1 तत् n1/1 एतत् n1/1 नान्दनम् n1/1 । तस्य m1/1 त्रयः m1/1 आवसथाः m1/1 त्रयः m1/1 स्वप्नाः m1/1 ।
अयम् m1/1 आवसथः m1/1 अयम् आवसथः m1/1 अयम् आवसथः m1/1 इति 0 ॥

सः He the great Soul एव as if एतम् सीमानं the sutures on the skull विदार्य having cut, एतया द्वारा by this door प्रापद्यत । entered.
सा एषा the द्वाः door is नाम named विदृतिः Vidriti = openable by special technique alone.
तत् एतत् नान्दनम् । it is blissful. (being able to reach this doorway, as yogis do in meditation).
तस्य of the Soul's त्रयः three आवसथाः resting places, त्रयः three स्वप्नाः । states of rest, are experienced.
अयम् आवसथः this place and state, अयम् आवसथः that place and state, अयम् आवसथः third place इति ॥ also.

**1.3.12** The safeguard to prevent accidental use and infringement is tabled. A nondescript and out of the limelight method is put in place. This ensures well-being, happiness, and relative peace of mind to the owner.

---

नान्दनम् = नन्दनम् । The long नकारः is Vedic usage.

द्वाः f1/1, द्वारा f3/1 from द्वार् ।

तस्य of the human consciousness

त्रयः three आवसथाः places within the body to be present without any doubt (1) senses (2) intellect (3) heart, and its corresponding त्रयः three स्वप्नाः states of presence (i) while waking in the senses (ii) while dreaming in the intellect (iii) while deep sleeping in the heart.

"Three Places Present" can also be interpreted as the three distinct phases of a human (a) in mother's womb (b) as his own normal self (c) as his father or son or family tree whomsoever society closely identifies him with.

---

Consciousness of each individual is bigger than the Body. For an analogy consider the consciousness as the flame around the body as a wick of a candle.

The **twinkle** in one's eye is the presence of consciousness. Similarly the fine **opinion** in the intellect and the powerful **emotion** in the heart are the reflections of one's consciousness.

स जातो भूतान्यभिव्यैख्यत् किमिहान्यं वावदिषदिति ।
स एतमेव पुरुषं ब्रह्म ततममपश्यत् । इदमदर्शमिती ३ ॥ १.३.१३

sa jāto bhūtānyabhivyaikhyat kimihānyaṃ vāvadiṣaditi |
sa etameva puruṣaṃ brahma tatamamapaśyat |
idamadarśamitī 3 || 1.3.13

सः$^{m1/1}$ जातः$^{m1/1}$ भूतानि$^{n2/3}$ अभिव्यैख्यत्$^{iii/1}$ लङ् किम्$^{n1/1}$ इह$^{0}$ अन्यं$^{n2/1}$ वावदिषत्$^{iii/1}$ सन् लङ् इति$^{0}$ ।
सः$^{m1/1}$ एतम्$^{m2/1}$ एव$^{0}$ पुरुषं$^{m2/1}$ ब्रह्म$^{n2/1}$ ततमम्$^{n2/1}$ अपश्यत्$^{iii/1}$ लङ् । इदम्$^{n1/1}$ अदर्शम्$^{i/1}$ लङ् इती ३ ॥

सः जातः He the one born भूतानि as the embodied beings अभिव्यैख्यत् and so known,
"इह किम् अन्यं here what else वावदिषत् may be said?" इति । thus contemplated.
सः पुरुषं He the (human embodied) soul एव एतम् only this ततमम् ब्रह्म अपश्यत् । ultimate Brahman saw.
इदम् अदर्शम् IT (the Brahman) "I (the seeker) have experienced", इती ३ ॥ proclaimed with lasting finality.

---

इती ३ ॥ Notice the प्लुतः pluta vowel ई ३ here. It is the mark of deep contemplation. Long silent meditation.

## 1.3.13 The Transcendent loves mystery.

The noble person remains out of the glare of society. The saint prefers not to reveal his powers to all.

Anything divine, anything sacred assumes the power of secrecy. It becomes hidden. It is never directly disclosed. It is not in public view. It cannot be common knowledge.

Then what is the answer? How can it be realized?

In Deep Meditation. By Dharana Dhyana Samadhi the seeker experiences the Divine.

- Dharana – a focus or contraction.
- Dhyana – letting go or expansion.
- Samadhi – deep restful meditation.

He gets a lasting vision of the ultimate reality. He proclaims it to himself. He announces not to the world outside, but to himself alone. This is not a verbal proclamation. It is simply an affirmation and assimilation deep inside the heart.

---

Patanjali Yoga Sutras. The Sanyam Course of the Art of Living Foundation.

तस्मादिदन्द्रो नामेदन्द्रो ह वै नाम । तमिदन्द्रं सन्तमिन्द्र इत्याचक्षते परोक्षेण । परोक्षप्रिया इव हि देवाः परोक्षप्रिया इव हि देवाः ॥ १.३.१४

tasmādidandro nāmedandro ha vai nāma I tamidandraṃ santamindra ityācakṣate parokṣeṇa I parokṣapriyā iva hi devāḥ parokṣapriyā iva hi devāḥ II 1.3.14

तस्मात्$^{0}$ इदन्द्रः$^{\text{m1/1}}$ नाम$^{\text{n1/1}}$ इदन्द्रः$^{\text{m1/1}}$ ह$^{0}$ वै$^{0}$ नाम$^{\text{n1/1}}$ । तम्$^{\text{m2/1}}$ इदन्द्रं$^{\text{m2/1}}$ सन्$^{\text{PrPA iii/1 शतृ}}$ तम्$^{\text{m2/1}}$ इन्द्रः$^{\text{m1/1}}$ इति$^{0}$ आचक्षते$^{\text{iii/3 लट्}}$ परोक्षेण$^{\text{n3/1}}$ । परोक्षप्रियाः$^{\text{m1/3}}$ इव$^{0}$ हि$^{0}$ देवाः$^{\text{m1/3}}$ परोक्षप्रियाः$^{\text{m1/3}}$ इव$^{0}$ हि$^{0}$ देवाः$^{\text{m1/3}}$ ॥

तस्मात् इदन्द्रः नाम Hence this-inward-seeing entity,
इदन्द्रः ह वै नाम । Indeed TurnedInward its name.
तम् इदन्द्रं सन् he (a seeker) on being Meditative,
"तम् he इन्द्रः Indra", इति thus परोक्षेण by meditation
आचक्षते । deeply visualize.
परोक्षप्रियाः इव हि देवाः the gods favor Deep Contemplation alone,
परोक्षप्रियाः इव हि देवाः ॥ the Divine Deities prefer anonymity, hence are beyond the grasp of senses, and cannot be proved nor disproved by logic.

---

इदन्द्रः Senses Turned Inward =
Sight lowered at angle of 30°.
Famous meditative posture of Gautama Buddha.

1.3.14 It has been the experience of all sages down the ages.

Controlling one's senses = Brahmacharya is a primary step for a sadhaka to attain final liberation.

Lord is invisible. Lord is beyond rhyme and reason.

Consciousness has been called by the names

- ब्रह्मा Vast, the infinite
- इन्द्र Senses Overlord, the balancer
- प्रजापति Emperor, the topmost ruler
- देवी–देवता Talents, the skills that give joy
- पञ्चमहाभूत Physics Chemistry Math

Consciousness takes birth by the routes

- उद्भिज Embryonic Womb
- स्वेदज Heat in Sweat
- अण्डज Egg
- जरायुज Shoot

# 2nd Chapter 1st Section

## The Story becomes Personal hence Real

So far we had opened our aperture wide, very wide. We took a bite of TIME SPACE with both arms.

Now we zoom and focus. We put the limelight on ourselves. We point a straight finger. Inwards.

पुरुषे ह वा अयमादितो गर्भो भवति ।
यदेतद्रेतस्तदेतत्सर्वेभ्योऽङ्गेभ्यस्तेजः सम्भूतमात्मन्येवाऽऽत्मानं बिभर्ति ।
तद् यदा स्त्रियां सिञ्चत्यथैनज्जनयति तदस्य प्रथमं जन्म ॥ २.१.१

puruṣe ha vā ayamādito garbho bhavati I yadetadretastadetatsarvebhyo'ṅgebhyastejaḥ sambhūtamātmanyevā''tmānaṃ bibharti I tad yadā striyāṃ siñcatyathainajjanayati tadasya prathamaṃ janma II 2.1.1

पुरुषे m7/1 ह 0 वै 0 अयम् m1/1 आदितः m1/1 गर्भः m1/1 भवति iii/1 लट् । यत् n1/1 एतत् n1/1 रेतः n1/1 तत् n2/1 एतत् n2/1 सर्वेभ्यः m5/3 अङ्गेभ्यः n5/3 तेजः n1/1 सम्भूतम् PPP n1/1 आत्मनि m7/1 एव 0 आत्मानं m2/1 बिभर्ति iii/1 लट् । तत् n1/1 यदा 0 स्त्रियां f7/1 सिञ्चति iii/1 लट् अथ 0 एनत् n2/1 जनयति iii/1 लट् तत् n1/1 अस्य m6/1 प्रथमं n1/1 जन्म n1/1 ॥

पुरुषे In the body of man ह वै *(spoken with seriousness and earnestness)* अयम् this आदितः initial गर्भः embryo भवति । is.
यत् What एतत् this रेतः sperm does is
तत् that एतत् it सर्वेभ्यः अङ्गेभ्यः from all organs तेजः vitality सम्भूतम् properly collects and
आत्मनि in its central core एव आत्मानं the packet of emotions and desires बिभर्ति । bears.
तत् That sperm यदा when स्त्रियां in the female सिञ्चति is inserted अथ then एनत् it जनयति procreates,
तत् that अस्य of it प्रथमं the common जन्म ॥ birth is.

### 2.1.1 Genetics

Common birth is one that is familiar to all.

We know the normal mechanism of love-making and reproduction.

What this verse adds is that the bundle of emotions-sensations-ambitions-convictions, all of it apart from the physical traits,

is also in the design blueprint of new birth.

---

A short course on genetic engineering.

तत् स्त्रिया आत्मभूयं गच्छति । यथा स्वमङ्गं तथा । तस्मादेनां न हिनस्ति । साऽस्यैतमात्मानमत्र गतं भावयति ॥ २.१.२

tat striyā ātmabhūyaṃ gacchati I yathā svamaṅgaṃ tathā I tasmādenāṃ na hinasti I sā'syaitamātmānamatra gataṃ bhāvayati II 2.1.2

तत् n1/1 स्त्रियाः f7/1 आत्मभूयं n1/1 गच्छति iii/1 लट् । यथा 0 स्वम् n1/1 अङ्गं n1/1 तथा 0 । तस्मात् 0 एनां f2/1 न 0 हिनस्ति iii/1 लट् । सा f1/1 अस्य m6/1 एतम् m2/1 आत्मानम् m2/1 अत्र 0 गतं PPP n1/1 भावयति iii/1 लट् ॥

तत् That sperm स्त्रियाः into the lady आत्मभूयं an intimate part गच्छति । becomes .
यथा स्वम् अङ्गं तथा । Just as her own body part.
तस्मात् एनां न हिनस्ति । Hence to her doesn't cause harm.
सा अस्य एतम् आत्मानम् गतं She of it like her own self treats, अत्र भावयति ॥. thereby nurtures.

### 2.1.2 Responsibility of Intimacy is Total

Of intimacy it is said, it becomes owned, it becomes very close, so dear that it is nurtured, taken care of exceedingly well.

Whatever one assumes ownership of, the responsibility taken for that is total.

सा भावयित्री भावयितव्या भवति । तं स्त्री गर्भं बिभर्ति । सोऽग्र एव कुमारं जन्मनोऽग्रेऽधिभावयति । स यत्कुमारं जन्मनोऽग्रेऽधिभावयत्यात्मानमेव तद्भावयत्येषां लोकानां सन्तत्या । एवं सन्तता हीमे लोकास्तदस्य द्वितीयं जन्म ॥ २.१.३

sā bhāvayitrī bhāvayitavyā bhavati । taṃ strī garbhaṃ bibharti । so'gra eva kumāraṃ janmano'gre'dhibhāvayati । sa yatkumāraṃ janmano'gre'dhibhāvayatyātmānameva tadbhāvayatyeṣāṃ lokānāṃ santatyā । evaṃ santatā hīme lokāstadasya dvitīyaṃ janma ॥ 2.1.3

सा [f1/1] भावयित्री [f1/1] भावयितव्या [f1/1] भवति [iii/1 लट्] । तं [m2/1] स्त्री [f1/1] गर्भं [m2/1] बिभर्ति [iii/1 लट्] । सः [m1/1] अग्रे [n7/1] एव [0] कुमारं [m2/1] जन्मनः [n6/1] अग्रे [n7/1] अधिभावयति [iii/1 लट्] । सः [m1/1] यत् [n1/1] कुमारं [m2/1] जन्मनः [n6/1] अग्रे [n7/1] अधिभावयति [iii/1 लट्] आत्मानम् [m2/1] एव [0] तत् [n1/1] भावयति [iii/1 लट्] एषां [m6/3] लोकानां [m6/3] सन्तत्या [f3/1] । एवं [0] सन्तताः [f1/3] हि [0] इमे [m1/3] लोकाः [m1/3] तत् [n1/1] अस्य [m6/1] द्वितीयं [n1/1] जन्म [n1/1] ॥

सा भावयित्री She the one carrying the baby भावयितव्या भवति । herself becomes the one who is to be exceptionally well taken care of.
तं स्त्री गर्भं बिभर्ति । That lady nurtures the embryo.
सः अग्रे एव कुमारं जन्मनः He (the father) also till the time of delivery, of the child in the womb अग्रे अधिभावयति । before and after the birth takes remarkable care.
सः यत् कुमारं जन्मनः अग्रे अधिभावयति The father of that child prior and post-delivery gives proper attention.

### 2.1.3 Specially Born to continue Legacy

The father of that child,
prior and post-delivery,
gives proper attention to detail.

Based on which talents are desirable,

- He accordingly maintains himself.
- He creates a suitable atmosphere for the pregnant mother.
- Both give particular attention to foods eaten, movies watched, songs played, conversations done.
- Yoga, Pranayama, soothing music, and reading and chanting of scriptures are especially favored.

आत्मानम् एव As one's own self तत् भावयति the child is reared, एषां लोकानां सन्तत्या । for continuity by the bloodline in these regions and cultures.

एवं सन्तताः हि इमे लोकाः Likewise that continuity of the lineage in these lands and peoples,
तत् अस्य that of it is द्वितीयं जन्म ॥ the special birth.

सोऽस्यायमात्मा पुण्येभ्यः कर्मभ्यः प्रतिधीयते । अथास्यायमितर आत्मा कृतकृत्यो वयोगतः प्रैति । स इतः प्रयन्नेव पुनर्जायते तदस्य तृतीयं जन्म ॥ २.१.४

so'syāyamātmā puṇyebhyaḥ karmabhyaḥ pratidhīyate I athāsyāyamitara ātmā kṛtakṛtyo vayogataḥ praiti I sa itaḥ prayanneva punarjāyate tadasya tṛtīyaṃ janma II 2.1.4

सः [m1/1] अस्य [m6/1] अयम् [m1/1] आत्मा [m1/1] पुण्येभ्यः [n5/3] कर्मभ्यः [n5/3] प्रतिधीयते [iii/1 लट्] । अथ [0] अस्य [m6/1] अयम् [m1/1] इतरः [0] आत्मा [m1/1] कृतकृत्यः [m1/1] वयोगतः [m1/1] प्रैति [iii/1 लट्] । सः [m1/1] इतः [0] प्रयन् [PrPA m1/1 शतृ] एव [0] पुनः [0] जायते [iii/1 लट्] तदस्य [m6/1] तृतीयं [n1/1] जन्म [n1/1] ॥

सः Man having done the job of giving birth and rearing अस्य अयम् आत्मा, his Soul now पुण्येभ्यः कर्मभ्यः प्रतिधीयते । turns towards meritorious and noble deeds.

अथ In due course of time अस्य अयम् इतरः आत्मा his other self i.e. the physical body कृतकृत्यः having fulfilled all responsibilities वयोगतः प्रैति । in the ripe old age departs.

सः Man इतः प्रयन् एव dropping this body forthwith पुनः जायते is reborn.

तदस्य Verily that of it is तृतीयं जन्म ॥ the undying birth.

---

तदस्य = तत् अस्य । Used as a compound word also.

### 2.1.4 The Undying Birth

The soul travels through bodies. It also travels through traits and virtues.

Since a Soul gets known and remembered in diverse ways

- Through physical lineage
- Through propagation of ideals
- Through celebration of festivals and anniversaries
- Some other means

Hence that is known as the Undying Birth.

तदुक्तमृषिणा गर्भे नु सन्नन्वेषामवेदमहं देवानां जनिमानि विश्वा । शतं मा पुर आयसीररक्षन्नधः श्येनो जवसा निरदीयमिति । गर्भ एवैतच्छयानो वामदेव एवमुवाच ॥ २.१.५

taduktamṛṣiṇā garbhe nu sannanveṣāmavedamahaṃ devānāṃ janimāni viśvā | śataṃ mā pura āyasīrarakṣannadhaḥ śyeno javasā niradīyamiti | garbha evaitacchayāno vāmadeva evamuvāca || 2.1.5

तत्[n1/1] उक्तम्[PPP n1/1] ऋषिणा[m3/1] गर्भे[m7/1] नु[0] सन्[PrPA m1/1 शतृ] अनु[0] एषाम्[m6/3] अवेदम्[i/1 लङ्] अहं[m1/1] देवानां[f6/3] जनिमानि[n2/3] विश्वा[f1/1] । शतं[n1/1] मा[m2/1] पुरः[f2/3] आयसीः[f2/3] अरक्षन्[iii/3 लङ्] अधः[0] श्येनः[m1/1] जवसा[n3/1] निरदीयम्[i/1] इति । गर्भे[m7/1] एव[0] एतत्[n1/1] शयानः[m1/1] वामदेवः[m1/1] एवम्[0] उवाच[iii/1 लिट्] ॥

तत् उक्तम् ऋषिणा Quote of a famous Sage,
अहं गर्भे नु सन् "Myself having been in womb(s)
अनु एषाम् अवेदम् and having minutely known these
देवानां जनिमानि विश्वा । godly births or worldly times,
शतं पुरः in a hundred cityBodies,
आयसीः अरक्षन् अधः ironlike protection nay imprison,
मा Myself श्येनः hawk-like जवसा in the twinkling of an eye निरदीयम् इति । rent it asunder".

---

मा mfn2/1 from अस्मद् । अहं mfn1/1 from अस्मद् ।
पुरः from पुर् ।

## 2.1.5 Vāmadeva Ṛṣi's Blessing

This is the story of an enlightened master. Its revelation has the power to release a human being's bonds.

It is a verse of great impact.
It has liberated many souls.

---

गर्भे एव एतत् शयानः As if resting in the womb, so the story goes, the great Rishi
वामदेवः एवम् उवाच ॥ Vamadeva thus affirmed.

स एवं विद्वानस्माच्छरीरभेदादूर्ध्व उत्क्रम्यामुष्मिन् स्वर्गे लोके सर्वान् कामानाप्त्वाऽमृतः समभवत् समभवत् ॥ २.१.६

sa evaṃ vidvānasmāccharīrabhedādūrdhva utkramyāmuṣmin svarge loke sarvān kāmānāptvā'mṛtaḥ samabhavat samabhavat || 2.1.6

सः एवं विद्वान् अस्मात् शरीर–भेदात् ऊर्ध्वः उत्क्रम्य अमुष्मिन् स्वर्गे लोके सर्वान् कामान् आप्त्वा अमृतः सम्–अभवत् सम्–अभवत् ॥

सः एवं विद्वान् He Vamadeva achieving this wisdom,
अस्मात् शरीर–भेदात् from this body getting liberated,
ऊर्ध्वः उत्क्रम्य rising beyond the gravity of the mortal plane,
अमुष्मिन् स्वर्गे लोके to the blissful heavenly plane,
सर्वान् कामान् आप्त्वा all plans having exhausted,
अमृतः सम्–अभवत् the nectar gained.
सम्–अभवत् ॥ He became united with the Eternal.

## 2.1.6 is a tour de force

and for all seekers a lighthouse.

How to be liberated? - By Letting Go. A recap of Origin, Infrastructure, Administration, Deities, Nourishment. Finally the Lord surveyed his handiwork. Something seems to be amiss he felt. “There should be a basic theme - a certain principle - that when applied would make it all meaningful to a discerning individual. Would establish him in dynamic harmony. Would give him a glimpse of deep peace. Of Bliss. Freedom. Nirvana”.

The ultimate beauty, the most precious love, the supremely desirable was not to be had by any of the senses. Not by sight, nor smell, nor hearing, nor taste, nor touch. Neither was it had by the intellect, nor by indulgence in procreation, nor by force of strength. Certainly not by plunging to death or engaging in injury to body or self.

By a grace and practice that energized the sahasrara chakra could the Brahman be united with. Could ultimate happiness result. However that couldn't be everyone's call. For everyone the Deep Sleep attribute was willed to give rest, a sense of peace, bliss, freedom. And this Shakti came to be called Indra - pacifier of mind and senses - giver of hope , and love, yet mysterious since sleep couldn't be brought on by will nor could it be denied if it came.

## 3rd Chapter 1st Section

### Freedom Mukti Nirvana

Contemplation and Deep Meditation lead man home.

कोऽयमात्मेति वयमुपास्महे । कतरः स आत्मा । येन वा पश्यति येन वा श्रृणोति येन वा गन्धानाजिघ्रति येन वा वाचं व्याकरोति येन वा स्वादु चास्वादु च विजानाति ॥ ३.१.१

ko'yamātmeti vayamupāsmahe I kataraḥ sa ātmā I yena vā paśyati yena vā śṛṇoti yena vā gandhānājighrati yena vā vācaṃ vyākaroti yena vā svādu cāsvādu ca vijānāti II 3.1.1

कः अयम् आत्मा इति वयम् उपास्महे । कतरः सः आत्मा । येन वा पश्यति येन वा श्रृणोति येन वा गन्धान् आजिघ्रति येन वा वाचं व्याकरोति येन वा स्वादु च अस्वादु च विजानाति ॥

कः "Who and What अयम् is this आत्मा Soul?" इति *quote* वयम् that we all उपास्महे I with so much sincerity seek, contemplate, and meditate upon.
कतरः सः आत्मा I Which of the two is the actual Soul?
येन वा पश्यति by which sees or
येन वा श्रृणोति by which hears or
येन वा गन्धान् आजिघ्रति by which fragrances smells or
येन वा वाचं व्याकरोति by which speech articulates or
येन वा स्वादु च अस्वादु च विजानाति by which the tasty and the bland especially knows?

### 3.1.1 In Peace, Man begins to Reflect

Man gets a moment of peace. The ambient stillness and the lack of active to-do lists, cause something Beautiful to happen.

When the external environment is calm, and the inner thought is peaceful, then the Magic happens.

Contemplation on the Supreme Divinity arises. Interest in the Bigness awakens.

यदेतद्धृदयं मनश्चैतत् । संज्ञानमाज्ञानं विज्ञानं प्रज्ञानं मेधा
दृष्टिर्धृतिर्मतिर्मनीषा जूतिः स्मृतिः सङ्कल्पः क्रतुरसुः कामो वश इति ।
सर्वाण्येवैतानि प्रज्ञानस्य नामधेयानि भवन्ति ॥ ३.१.२

yadetaddhṛdayaṃ manaścaitat | saṃjñānamājñānaṃ vijñānaṃ prajñānaṃ medhā dṛṣṭirdhṛtirmatirmanīṣā jūtiḥ smṛtiḥ saṅkalpaḥ kraturasuḥ kāmo vaśa iti |

sarvāṇyevaitāni prajñānasya nāmadheyāni bhavanti || 3.1.2

यत् एतत् हृदयं मनः च एतत् । संज्ञानम् आज्ञानं विज्ञानं प्रज्ञानं मेधा दृष्टिः धृतिः मतिः मनीषा जूतिः स्मृतिः सङ्कल्पः क्रतुः असुः कामः वशः इति । सर्वाणि एव एतानि प्रज्ञानस्य नामधेयानि भवन्ति ॥

यत् एतत् हृदयं मनः च What rules the Heart, the same governs the Mind as well.
एतत् It is
संज्ञानम् proper knowledge आज्ञानं orderly knowledge विज्ञानं scientific knowledge प्रज्ञानं awakened knowledge, also the same expresses as
मेधा intelligence दृष्टिः insight धृतिः perseverance मतिः sound opinion मनीषा freedom of thought जूतिः shyness स्मृतिः clear memory सङ्कल्पः strong decision क्रतुः earnestness असुः quiver free breath कामः वशः to have and own the desirable इति etc.
सर्वाणि एव एतानि All indeed these
प्रज्ञानस्य of the Consciousness
नामधेयानि various names भवन्ति ॥ are.

### 3.1.2 All Noble Qualities are Its Reflection

Now we see the whole gamut of noble virtues and qualities as being a reflection of the Supreme alone.

एष ब्रह्मैष इन्द्र एष प्रजापतिरेते सर्वे देवा इमानि च पञ्च महाभूतानि पृथिवी वायुराकाश आपो ज्योतींषीत्येतानीमानि च क्षुद्रमिश्राणीव । बीजानीतराणि चेतराणि चाण्डजानि च जारुजानि च स्वेदजानि चोद्भिजानि चाश्वा गावः पुरुषा हस्तिनो यत्किञ्चेदं प्राणि जङ्गमं च पतत्रि च यच्च स्थावरं सर्वं तत्प्रज्ञानेत्रम् । प्रज्ञाने प्रतिष्ठितं प्रज्ञानेत्रो लोकः प्रज्ञा प्रतिष्ठा प्रज्ञानं ब्रह्म ॥ ३.१.३

eṣa brahmaiṣa indra eṣa prajāpatirete sarve devā imāni ca pañca mahābhūtāni pṛthivī vāyurākāśa āpo jyotīṃṣītyetānīmāni ca kṣudramiśrāṇīva I bījānītarāṇi cetarāṇi cāṇḍajāni ca jārujāni ca svedajāni codbhijāni cāśvā gāvaḥ puruṣā hastino yatkiñcedaṃ prāṇi jaṅgamaṃ ca patatri ca yacca sthāvaraṃ sarvaṃ tatprajñānetram I prajñāne pratiṣṭhitaṃ prajñānetro lokaḥ prajñā pratiṣṭhā prajñānaṃ brahma II 3.1.3

एषः ब्रह्मा एषः इन्द्रः एषः प्रजापतिः एते सर्वे देवाः इमानि च पञ्च महाभूतानि पृथिवी वायुः आकाशः आपः ज्योतींषि इति एतानि इमानि च क्षुद्र–मिश्राणि इव । बीजानि इतराणि च इतराणि च अण्डजानि च जारुजानि च स्वेदजानि च उद्भिजानि च अश्वाः गावः पुरुषाः हस्तिनः यत् किञ्च इदं प्राणि जङ्गमं च पतत्रि च यत् च स्थावरं सर्वं तत् प्रज्ञानेत्रम् । प्रज्ञाने प्रतिष्ठितं प्रज्ञानेत्रः लोकः प्रज्ञा प्रतिष्ठा प्रज्ञानं ब्रह्म ॥

ज्योतींषि n1/3 from ज्योतिस् ।

प्राणि n1/1 from प्राणिन् ।

### 3.1.3 Maha Vakya – प्रज्ञानं ब्रह्म

prajñānaṃ brahma प्रज्ञानं ब्रह्म
Consciousness = Brahman.
Life = Divine.
Living = Respectable.

A verse of supreme understanding. An Enlightened statement.

एषः ब्रह्मा एषः इन्द्रः एषः प्रजापतिः This me within is Brahma = the Vast Infinity, is Indra = Lord of Senses, is Prajapati = the Lord of all Beings.
एते सर्वे देवाः It is these all deities = skills and talents.

इमानि च पञ्च महाभूतानि पृथिवी वायुः आकाशः आपः ज्योतींषि And is the five great elements – Earth, Air, Space, Water, and the Lights.

एतानि इमानि च क्षुद्र–मिश्राणि इव It is like a judicious mix of many small things, various virtues and attributes. It covers the spectrum of all insignificant creatures like bacteria and virus, ant and scorpion.

बीजानि इतराणि च इतराणि च अण्डजानि च जारुजानि च स्वेदजानि च उद्भिजानि Whether born of seed, or else of egg, or womb, or sweat-heat, or shoot
च अश्वाः गावः पुरुषाः हस्तिनः And Horses, Cows, Humans, Elephants.

यत् किञ्च इदं प्राणि Whatever that breathes e.g.

जङ्गमं च पतत्रि च having feet, having wing, यत् च स्थावरं and whatever immobile;

सर्वं तत् प्रज्ञा-नेत्रम् all that is Consciousness-Led. Willed by the Supreme.

प्रज्ञाने प्रतिष्ठितं in consciousness rooted,

प्रज्ञानेत्रः लोकः a consciously-dictated world

प्रज्ञा प्रतिष्ठा consciously supported.

प्रज्ञानं ब्रह्म Consciousness = Brahman.

prajñānaṃ brahma प्रज्ञानं ब्रह्म

प्रज्ञानं ब्रह्म Consciousness = Brahman.

स एतेन प्रज्ञेनाऽऽत्मनाऽस्माल्लोकादुत्क्रम्यामुष्मिन् स्वर्गे लोके सर्वान् कामानाप्त्वाऽमृतः समभवत् समभवत् ॥ ३.१.४

sa etena prajñenā''tmanā'smāllokādutkramyāmuṣmin svarge loke sarvān kāmānāptvā'mṛtaḥ samabhavat samabhavat || 3.1.4

सः एतेन प्रज्ञेन आत्मना अस्मात् लोकात् उत्क्रम्य अमुष्मिन् स्वर्गे लोके सर्वान् कामान् आप्त्वा अमृतः सम्–अभवत् सम्–अभवत् ॥

सः m1/1 He एतेन m3/1 प्रज्ञेन m3/1 आत्मना m3/1 by this conscious soul अस्मात् m5/1 लोकात् m5/1 from this worldly struggles plane उत्क्रम्य 0 gerund ल्यप् having broken free अमुष्मिन् m7/1 स्वर्गे m7/1 लोके m7/1 in this heavenly blissful plane सर्वान् m2/3 कामान् m2/3 आप्त्वा 0 gerund क्त्वा all aims having fulfilled and taken care of
अमृतः PPP m1/1 सम्–अभवत् iii/1 लङ् immortality duly-attained.
सम्–अभवत् ॥ Man became fully immortal, all pervasive, reposed in the Self.

### 3.1.4 O! Such fabulous wealth

What a joy to behold the nectar within. What blissful charm to be acquainted with the inner strength.

What greatness can equal the purity and humility of the Soul of Man?

Such a treasure. O! Such fabulous wealth.

Indeed fortunate is the man who glimpses his inner space. The space that is divine, whole, and without lack. The part of him that is God, Godly, Godliness.

---

We are all Conscious. We are all a reflection of the Supreme Consciousness.

We are all Brahman.
i.e.
We are all Eternal, Imperishable, Blissful, Divine.

Aitareya ends on this decisive happy note.

# Etymology of Upanishad

व्युत्पत्ति
Consider Adi Shankaracharya's derivation of the word 'Upanishad' as given in his bhashyam on the Katha Upanishad.

उप + नि + षद् + क्विप् –> उपनिषद्

The Sanskrit root from Dhatupatha 1c - 854, 6c - 1427 षद्ऌ विशरण–गति–अवसादनेषु has the three meanings, namely विशरण= wither, गति= attain, अवसादनं = sit.

In the context of wisdom, we can say

- wither away one's stupidity
- attain liberation
- sit with a conviction

The upasarga उप stands for nearness, closeness.

The upasarga नि stands for delving into, intensely.

The pratyaya क्विप् makes a noun, and while joining, it vanishes entirely.

Thus the word 'Upanishad' is formed, and it has the meaning of destroying one's ignorance and gaining freedom, when we sit devotedly at the feet of the Master.

# Latin Transliteration Chart

International Alphabet of Sanskrit Transliteration (I.A.S.T.)

| a | ā | i | ī | u | ū | ṛ | ṝ | ḷ | |
|---|---|---|---|---|---|---|---|---|---|
| अ | आ | इ | ई | उ | ऊ | ऋ | ॠ | ऌ | |
| | | | | | | ृ | ॄ | ॢ | |
| e | ai | o | au | ṃ | m̐ | ḥ | Ardha Visarga | oṃ | |
| ए | ऐ | ओ | औ | ं | ँ | ः | □ | ॐ | |
| Consonants are shown with vowel 'a= अ' for uttering | | | | | | | | | |
| ka | क | ca | च | ṭa | ट | ta | त | pa | प |
| kha | ख | cha | छ | ṭha | ठ | tha | थ | pha | फ |
| ga | ग | ja | ज | ḍa | ड | da | द | ba | ब |
| gha | घ | jha | झ | ḍha | ढ | dha | ध | bha | भ |
| ṅa | ङ | ña | ञ | ṇa | ण | na | न | ma | म |
| | | | | | | | | | |
| ya | ra | la | va | | ḷa | ' | | | |
| य | र | ल | व | | ळ | ऽ | | | |
| | | | | | Consonant only | | | | |
| śa | ṣa | sa | ha | | ka | क्अ = क | | | |
| श | ष | स | ह | | k | क् | | | |

The symbol ᳲ is pronounced as गुं guṃ. It is an ayogavaha अयोगवाह sound seen in Vedic literature due to Sandhi.

# Verses for Chanting with Svara

Accents used in Sanskrit verses increase the power and flow of the mantras during chanting.

Anudatta ◌॒= अनुदात्तः = signifies base pitch.

Udatta = उदात्तः = unmarked, standard pitch.

Svarita ॑ = स्वरितः = high pitch.

Dirgha Svarita ᳚ =दीर्घः स्वरितः=high to low to normal pitch

॥ अथ ऋग्वेदीय ऐतरेयोपनिषद् ॥

शान्तिपाठः

ॐ वाङ् मे॒ मन॑सि प्रति॑ष्ठिता॒ । मनो॑ मे॒ वाचि॒ प्रति॑ष्ठितम् । आ॒विरा॒वीर्म॑

एधि । वे॒दस्य म॒ आणी᳚स्थः। श्रु॒तं मे॒ मा प्रहा॑सीः।

अ॒ने॒नाधीते॑नाहोरा॒त्रान् सन्द॑धामि । ऋ॒तं व॑दिष्यामि॒ । स॒त्यं व॑दिष्यामि॒

। तन्माम् अ॑वतु । तद् व॒क्तारम् अ॑व॒तु । अव॑तु॒ माम् । अव॑तु व॒क्ता॒रम्

अव॑तु व॒क्तारम्᳚ ॥ ॐ शान्ति॒ः शान्ति॒ः शान्ति॑ः ॥

<u>प्रथमोध्यायः प्रथमः खण्डः</u> ॐ

आत्मा वा इदमेक एवा᳚ग्र आसीन् नान्यत् किञ्चन मि॒षत् ।

स ईक्षत लोकान् नु सृ॑जा इ॒ति ॥ १.१.१

स इ॒माँल्लोकान् असृजत । अम्भो मरीचीर्मरमा᳚पोऽदो॒ऽम्भः परेण दि॒वं

द्यौः प्रतिष्ठा᳚ऽन्तरि॑क्षं मरी॒चयः पृ॒थिवी मरो या अ॒धस्तात्ता आ॒पः ॥

१.१.२

स ईक्षतेमे नु लोका लोकपालान् नु सृ॑जा इ॒ति । सोऽद्भ्य एव पु॒रुषं

समुद्धृत्या᳚मूर्च्छ॒यत् ॥ १.१.३

तमभ्य॑तपत्तस्याभितप्तस्य मुखं निर॑भि॒द्यत यथाऽण्डं मुखाद्

वाग्वाचो᳚ऽग्निर्ना॑सिके निर॑भिद्येतां नासिकाभ्यां प्रा॒णः ।

प्राणाद् वायुरक्षिणी निरभिद्येतामक्षिभ्यां चक्षुश्चक्षुष आदित्यः कर्णौ निरभिद्येतां कर्णाभ्यां श्रोत्रं श्रोत्राद्दिशस्त्वङ् निरभिद्यत त्वचो लोमानि लोमभ्य ओषधिवनस्पतयो हृदयं निरभिद्यत हृदयान्मनो मनसश्चन्द्रमा नाभिर्निरभिद्यत नाभ्या अपानोऽपानान्मृत्युः शिश्नं निरभिद्यत शिश्नाद्रेतो रेतस आपः ॥ १.१.४

प्रथमोध्यायः द्वितीयः खण्डः

ता एता देवताः सृष्टा अस्मिन् महत्यर्णवे प्रापतंस्तमशनाया-पिपासाभ्यामन्ववार्जत् । ता एनमब्रुवन्नायतनं नः प्रजानीहि यस्मिन् प्रतिष्ठिता अन्नमदामेति ॥ १.२.१

ताभ्यो गामानयत्ता अब्रुवन्न वै नोऽयमलमिति ।
ताभ्योऽश्वमानयत्ता अब्रुवन्न वै नोऽयमलमिति ॥ १.२.२

ताभ्यः पुरुषमानयत्ता अब्रुवन् सुकृतं बतेति । पुरुषो वाव सुकृतम् । ता अब्रवीद्यथायतनं प्रविशतेति ॥ १.२.३

अग्निर्वाग्भूत्वा मुखं प्राविशद् वायुः प्राणो भूत्वा नासिके प्राविशदादित्यश्चक्षुर्भूत्वा अक्षिणी प्राविशद्दिशः श्रोत्रं भूत्वा कर्णौ प्राविशन्नोषधिवनस्पतयो लोमानि भूत्वा त्वचं प्राविशंश्चन्द्रमा मनो भूत्वा हृदयं प्राविशन्मृत्युरपानो भूत्वा नाभिं प्राविशदापो रेतो भूत्वा शिश्नं प्राविशन् ॥ १.२.४

तमशनायापिपासे अब्रूतामावाभ्यामभिप्रजानीहीति । ते अब्रवीदेतास्वेव वां देवतास्वाभजाम्येतासु भागिन्यौ करोमीति । तस्माद् यस्यै कस्यै च देवतायै हविर्गृह्यते भागिन्यावेवास्यामशनायापिपासे भवतः ॥ १.२.५

प्रथमोध्यायः तृतीयः खण्डः

स ईक्षतेमे नु लोकाश्च लोकपालाश्चान्नमेभ्यः सृजा इति ॥ १.३.१

सोऽपोऽभ्यतपत् ताभ्योऽभितप्ताभ्यो मूर्तिरजायत ।
या वै सा मूर्तिरजायतान्नं वै तत् ॥ १.३.२
तदेनत्सृष्टं पराङत्यजिघांसत् । तद् वाचाऽजिघृक्षत् तन्नाशक्नोद्वाचा
ग्रहीतुम् । स यद्धैनद्वाचाऽग्रहैष्यदभिव्याहृत्य हैवान्नमत्रप्स्यत् ॥ १.३.३
तत् प्राणेनाजिघृक्षत् तन्नाशक्नोत् प्राणेन ग्रहीतुम् ।
स यद्धैनत्प्राणेनाग्रहैष्यदभिप्राण्य हैवान्नमत्रप्स्यत् ॥ १.३.४
तच् चक्षुषाऽजिघृक्षत् तन्नाशक्नोच्चक्षुषा ग्रहीतुम् ।
स यद्धैनच्चक्षुषाऽग्रहैष्यद् दृष्ट्वा हैवान्नमत्रप्स्यत् ॥ १.३.५
तच्छ्रोत्रेणाजिघृक्षत् तन्नाशक्नोच्छ्रोत्रेण ग्रहीतुम् ।
स यद्धैनच्छ्रोत्रेणाग्रहैष्यच्छ्रुत्वा हैवान्नमत्रप्स्यत् ॥ १.३.६
तत् त्वचाऽजिघृक्षत् तन्नाशक्नोत्त्वचा ग्रहीतुम् ।
स यद्धैनत्त्वचाऽग्रहैष्यत् स्पृष्ट्वा हैवान्नमत्रप्स्यत् ॥ १.३.७
तन्मनसाऽजिघृक्षत् तन्नाशक्नोन्मनसा ग्रहीतुम् ।
स यद्धैनन्मनसाऽग्रहैष्यद् ध्यात्वा हैवान्नमत्रप्स्यत् ॥ १.३.८
तच्छिश्नेनाजिघृक्षत् तन्नाशक्नोच्छिश्नेन ग्रहीतुम् ।
स यद्धैनच्छिश्नेनाग्रहैष्यद् विसृज्य हैवान्नमत्रप्स्यत् ॥ १.३.९
तदपानेनाजिघृक्षत् तदावयत् ।
सैषोऽन्नस्य ग्रहो यद् वायुरन्नायुर्वा एष यद्वायुः ॥ १.३.१०
स ईक्षत कथं न्विदं मदृते स्यादिति स ईक्षत कतरेण प्रपद्या इति ।
स ईक्षत यदि वाचाऽभिव्याहृतं यदि प्राणेनाभिप्राणितं यदि चक्षुषा दृष्टं
यदि श्रोत्रेण श्रुतं यदि त्वचा स्पृष्टं यदि मनसा ध्यातं
यद्यपानेनाभ्यपानितं यदि शिश्नेन विसृष्टमथ कोऽहमिति ॥ १.३.११
स एतमेव सीमानं विदार्यैतया द्वारा प्रापद्यत। सैषा विदृतिर्नाम
द्वास्तदेतन्नान्दनम्। तस्य त्रय आवसथास्त्रयः स्वप्नाः ।
अयमावसथोऽयमावसथोऽयमावसथ इति ॥ १.३.१२

स जातो भूतान्यभिव्यैख्यत् किमिहान्यं वावदिषदिति ।
स एतमेव पुरुषं ब्रह्म ततममपश्यत् । इदमदर्शनमिती ३ ॥ १.३.१३
तस्मादिदन्द्रो नामेदन्द्रो ह वै नाम । तमिदंन्द्रं सन्तमिन्द्र ईत्याचक्षते
परोक्षेण । परोक्षप्रिया इव हि देवाः परोक्षप्रिया इव हि देवाः ॥ १.३.१४

द्वितीयोध्यायः प्रथमः खण्डः

पुरुषे ह वा अयमादितो गर्भो भवति ।
यदेतद्रेतस्तदेतत्सर्वेभ्योऽङ्गेभ्यस्तेजः सम्भूतमात्मन्येवाऽऽत्मानं बिभर्ति
। तद् यदा स्त्रियां सिञ्चत्यथैनज्जनयति तदस्य प्रथमं जन्म ॥ २.१.१
तत् स्त्रिया आत्मभूयं गच्छति । यथा स्वमङ्गं तथा । तस्मादेनां न
हिनस्ति।
साऽस्यैतमात्मानमत्र गतं भावयति ॥ २.१.२
सा भावयित्री भावयितव्या भवति । तं स्त्री गर्भं बिभर्ति । सोऽग्र एव
कुमारं जन्मनोऽग्रेऽधिभावयति । स यत्कुमारं
जन्मनोऽग्रेऽधिभावयत्यात्मानमेव तद्भावयत्येषां लोकानां सन्तत्या ।
एवं सन्तता हीमे लोकास्तदस्य द्वितीयं जन्म ॥ २.१.३
सोऽस्यायमात्मा पुण्येभ्यः कर्मभ्यः प्रतिधीयते । अथास्यायमितर
आत्मा कृतकृत्यो वयोगतः प्रैति । स इतः प्रयन्नेव पुनर्जायते तदस्य
तृतीयं जन्म ॥ २.१.४
तदुक्तमृषिणा गर्भे नु सन्नन्वेषामवेदमहं देवानां जनिमानि विश्वा । शतं
मा पुर आयसीररक्षन्नधः श्येनो जवसा निरदीयमिति । गर्भ
एवैतच्छयानो वामदेव एवमुवाच ॥ २.१.५
स एवं विद्वानस्माच्छरीरभेदादूर्ध्व उत्क्रम्यामुष्मिन् स्वर्गे लोके सर्वान्
कामानाप्त्वाऽमृतः समभवत् समभवत् ॥ २.१.६

तृतीयोध्यायः प्रथमः खण्डः

कोऽयमात्मेति वयमुपास्महे । कतरः स आत्मा । येन वा पश्यति येन
वा शृणोति येन वा गन्धानाजिघ्रति येन वा वाचं व्याकरोति येन वा स्वादु
चास्वादु च विजानाति ॥ ३.१.१

यदेतद्धृदयं मनश्चैतत् । संज्ञानमाज्ञानं विज्ञानं प्रज्ञानं मेधा
दृष्टिर्धृतिर्मतिर्मनीषा जूतिः स्मृतिः सङ्कल्पः क्रतुरसुः कामो वश इति ।
सर्वाण्येवैतानि प्रज्ञानस्य नामधेयानि भवन्ति ॥ ३.१.२

एष ब्रह्मैष इन्द्र एष प्रजापतिरेते सर्वे देवा इमानि च पञ्च महाभूतानि
पृथिवी वायुराकाश आपो ज्योतींषीत्येतानीमानि च क्षुद्रमिश्राणीव ।
बीजानीतराणि चेतराणि चाण्डजानि च जारुजानि च स्वेदजानि
चोद्भिजानि चाश्वा गावः पुरुषा हस्तिनो यत्किञ्चेदं प्राणि जङ्गमं च
पतत्रि च यच्च स्थावरं सर्वं तत्प्रज्ञानेत्रम् । प्रज्ञाने प्रतिष्ठितं प्रज्ञानेत्रो
लोकः प्रज्ञा प्रतिष्ठा प्रज्ञानं ब्रह्म ॥ ३.१.३

स एतेन प्रज्ञेनाऽऽत्मनाऽस्माल्लोकादुत्क्रम्यामुष्मिन् स्वर्गे लोके सर्वान्
कामानाप्त्वाऽमृतः समभवत् समभवत् ॥ ३.१.४

॥ इति ऐतरेयोपनिषत् समाप्ता ॥

ॐ वाङ् मे मनसि प्रतिष्ठिता । मनो मे वाचि प्रतिष्ठितम् । आविरावीर्मं
एधि । वेदस्य म आणीस्थः। श्रुतं मे मा प्रहासीः।
अनेनाधीतेनाहोरात्रान् सन्दधामि । ऋतं वदिष्यामि । सत्यं वदिष्यामि
। तन्माम् अवतु । तद् वक्तारम् अवतु । अवतु माम् । अवतु वक्तारम्
अवतु वक्तारम् ॥ ॐ शान्तिः शान्तिः शान्तिः ॥

# Sanskrit Grammar

Sandhis separated word by word पदच्छेद (प०), Verses in prose order अन्वय (अ०),and with विभक्ति Cases.

Abbreviations

Nouns

m masculine, f feminine, n neuter; V vocative
1/1 = vibhakti case from 1 to 7/number 1 to 3

Indeclinables (uninflected nouns or verbs) 0
In Sanskrit the **adverbs** are mostly uninflected.

Verbs

iii/1 = person i to iii / number 1 to 3
PPP = Past Participle Passive = क्त
PPA = Past Participle Active = क्तवत्
PrPA = PresentParticiple Active = शतृ/ शानच्
PoPP = PotentialParticiple Passive = य, तव्य, अनीयर् (gerund)
तुमुन् = infinitive, in the sense of "to do"

Anusvara and Makara have been kept as they are in Padacheda, to avoid over work. E.g. इदं should be written as इदम् in Padacheda.
Sanskrit Literature frequently omits the verb – "is". The words भवति, अस्ति etc. are implicit.
E.g. 2.1.1 तत् अस्य प्रथमं जन्म ॥ (भवति)

Since Sanskrit is an inflectional language, the **spelling of the same word** changes as per context or usage. Hence words can be **placed anywhere** in a sentence, as in poetic use, without change in meaning. The matrix shows how.

### Verb inflections in Sanskrit – a sample chart

| 982 गमॢ गतौ – to go, also in the sense of attainment | | | |
|---|---|---|---|
| Present Tense Active voice लट् कर्त्तरि प्रयोगः | | | |
| Person/no | singular | dual | plural |
| Third | गच्छति[iii/1] | गच्छतः[iii/2] | गच्छन्ति[iii/3] |
| Second | गच्छसि[ii/1] | गच्छथः[ii/2] | गच्छथ [ii/3] |
| First | गच्छामि[i/1] | गच्छावः [i/2] | गच्छामः[i/3] |

### Noun declensions in Sanskrit – a sample chart

| Masculine stem, vowel अending | | | |
|---|---|---|---|
| (र्–आ–म्–अ) राम[m] Lord's name | | | |
| | singular[1] | dual [2] | plural [3] |
| 1 Doer | रामः[1/1] | रामौ[1/2] | रामाः[1/3] |
| 2 Object | रामम्[2/1] | रामौ[2/2] | रामान्[2/3] |
| 3 by | रामेण[3/1] | रामाभ्याम्[3/2] | रामैः[3/3] |
| 4 for | रामाय[4/1] | रामाभ्याम्[4/2] | रामेभ्यः[4/3] |
| 5 from | रामात्[5/1] | रामाभ्याम् [5/2] | रामेभ्यः[5/3] |
| 6 of | रामस्य[6/1] | रामयोः[6/2] | रामाणाम्[6/3] |
| 7 in | रामे[7/1] | रामयोः[7/2] | रामेषु[7/3] |
| Vocative | हे राम[V/1] | हे रामौ[V/2] | हे रामाः[V/3] |

| Masculine stem, consonant त् ending | | | |
|---|---|---|---|
| मरुत्$^{m}$ Wind, Breeze, Air | | | |
| | singular[1] | dual [2] | plural [3] |
| 1 Doer | मरुत् $^{1/1}$ | मरुतौ $^{1/2}$ | मरुतः $^{1/3}$ |
| 2 Object | मरुतम् $^{2/1}$ | मरुतौ $^{2/2}$ | मरुतः $^{2/3}$ |
| 3 by | मरुता $^{3/1}$ | मरुद्भ्याम् $^{3/2}$ | मरुद्भिः $^{3/3}$ |
| 4 for | मरुते $^{4/1}$ | मरुद्भ्याम् $^{4/2}$ | मरुद्भ्यः $^{4/3}$ |
| 5 from | मरुतः $^{5/1}$ | मरुद्भ्याम् $^{5/2}$ | मरुद्भ्यः $^{5/3}$ |
| 6 of | मरुतः $^{6/1}$ | मरुतोः $^{6/2}$ | मरुताम् $^{6/3}$ |
| 7 in | मरुति $^{7/1}$ | मरुतोः $^{7/2}$ | मरुत्सु $^{7/3}$ |
| Vocative | हे मरुत् $^{V/1}$ | हे मरुतौ $^{V/2}$ | हे मरुतः $^{V/3}$ |

Moods and Tenses in Sanskrit

| | | |
|---|---|---|
| 1 | लट् | Present Tense |
| 2 | लुङ् | Aorist Past Tense, *before from now onwards* |
| 3 | लङ् | Imperfect Past Tense – *before from yesterday onwards* |
| 4 | लिट् | Perfect Past Tense – *distant unseen past* |
| 5 | लृट् | Simple Future Tense – *now onwards* |
| 6 | लुट् | Periphrastic Future Tense – *tomorrow onwards* |
| 7 | लृङ् | Conditional Mood - *if/then in past or future* |
| 8 | लोट् | Imperative Mood – *request* |
| 9 | विधि–लिङ् | Potential Mood – *order विधिलिङ्* (also known as Optative Mood) |
| 10 | आशीर्–लिङ् | Benedictive Mood – *blessing आशीर्लिङ्* (also used in the sense of a curse) |

# Conjugation process of Verb

वदन्ति = they say, they describe.

1st conjugation Root, Parasmaipadi.

1009 √ वदँ व्यक्तायां वाचि । to tell, relate, describe.

1.3.1 भूवादयो धातवः। वदँ = वद्अँ ।

1.3.2 उपदेशेऽजनुनासिक इत् । 1.3.9 तस्य लोपः। वद् ।

3.4.69 लः कर्मणि च भावे चाकर्मकेभ्यः। वद् ।

3.2.123 वर्तमाने लट् । 3.4.77 लस्य । वद् + लँट् ।

1.3.3 हलन्त्यम् । 1.3.9 तस्य लोपः । वद्+लँ ।

1.3.2 उपदेशेऽजनुनासिक इत् । 1.3.9तस्य लोपः । वद्+ल् ।

3.4.78 तिप्तस्झिसिप्थस्थमिब्वस्मस् तातांझथासाथांध्वमिड्वहिमहिङ् ।

1.4.199 लः परस्मैपदम् । choose Parasmaipada affix.

वद्+झि । we are conjugating third person

1.4.101 तिङस्त्रीणि त्रीणि प्रथममध्यमोत्तमाः ।

1.4.102 तान्येकवचनद्विवचनबहुवचनान्येकशः । वद्+झि । plural

1.4.108 शेषे प्रथमः । वद्+झि । this is called "प्रथमः" i.e. the **first and most** used in language, third person.

3.4.113 तिङ्शित्सार्वधातुकम् । वद्+झि ।

3.1.68 कर्त्तरि शप् । वद्+शप्+झि ।

3.4.113तिङ्शित्सार्वधातुकम् । वद्+शप्+झि ।

7.1.3 झोऽन्तः । वद्+शप्+ अन्ति ।

1.3.3 हलन्त्यम्। 1.3.8लशक्वतद्धिते। 1.3.9तस्य लोपः।वद्+अ+अन्ति ।

6.1.97 अतो गुणे । वद्+अन्ति । sandhi drops the अकारः ।

8.3.24 नश्चापदान्तस्य झलि । वद् + अंति । Anusvara appears

8.4.58 अनुस्वारस्य ययि परसवर्णः । वद् + अन्ति ।

Anusvara again changes to नकारः ।

वद् + अन्ति = वदन्ति iii/3 लट् । iii = 3rd person, 3 = plural.

Third person plural, Present Tense.

## Declension process of Noun

ब्रह्म = Brahma. The Lord. Highest Intelligence.

Stem Brahmanब्रह्मन् n $\longrightarrow$ ब्रह्म neuter Nominative $^{1/1}$

The Great Lord. The Invisible presence.

1.2.45 अर्थवदधातुरप्रत्ययः प्रातिपदिकम् । ब्रह्मन्

1.2.46 कृत्तद्धितसमासाश्च । 3.1.1 प्रत्ययः । 3.1.2 परश्च ।

4.1.1 ङ्याप्प्रातिपदिकात् । 4.1.2 स्वौजस-

मौट्छष्टाभ्याम्भिस्ङेभ्याम्भ्यस्ङसिभ्याम्भ्यस्ङसोसाम्ङ्योस्सुप् ।

1.4.104विभक्तिश्च । 1.4.103 सुपः = use one of these vibhakti suffix. ब्रह्मन् + सुँ ।

1.4.22 द्व्येकयोर्द्विवचनैकवचने = singular number taken.

ब्रह्मन् + सुँ ।

7.1.23 स्वमोर्नपुंसकात् । 2.4.13 यस्मात्प्रत्ययविधिस्तदादि प्रत्ययेऽङ्गम् । 6.4.1 अङ्गस्य । 1st and 2nd case Vibhakti drops for neuter stem. ब्रह्मन् ।

1.4.17 स्वादिष्वसर्वनामस्थाने । The word gets पदसंज्ञा ।

ब्रह्मन् ।

8.2.7 न लोपः प्रातिपदिकान्तस्य । Final नकार drops.

ब्रह्म $^{n1/1}$ ।

*Neuter. First case nominative singular.* **Brahma**. The Highest. The Supreme. Shiva. Purusha. Tao. The Beautiful, The Love, The Infinite, The Divine. Any name is **Him**.

All directions point to **It**. Every form is **She**.

# References

https://www.ashtangayoga.info/philosophy/sanskrit-and-devanagari/transliteration-tool/
http://spokensanskrit.org/
https://upanishads.org.in/
https://www.academia.edu/31914623/Aitareya_Upanishad_Word-for-Word_Translation_with_Transliteration_and_Grammatical_Notes
http://vedicheritage.gov.in/brahmanas/aitareya-brahmana/

Audio Chant
https://www.youtube.com/watch?v=HoZJyctrR78

Guided Meditations Sri Sri Ravi Shankar
https://www.youtube.com/playlist?list=PL480C9CCB94DF5D82

- Hari Narayan Apte ऐतरेयारण्यकम् – 1st - 1898- Anandashram Printers, Poona.
- Jamuna Pathak ऐतरेयारण्यकम् – 1st Chaukhamba Krishnadas Academy, Varanasi.
- Various – ऐतरेयोपनिषद् सानुवाद शाङ्करभाष्यसहित – 1st - 1938 – Gita Press, Gorakhpur.
- Umeshanand Shastri – ऐतरेयोपनिषत् – 1st - 2000 – Kailash Ashram, Rishikesh.
- Swami Sarvananda – Aitareyopanishad – Reprint – 2005 - Sri Ramakrishna Math, Madras. (also kindle eBook)
- KLV Sastry & Anantarama Sastri – Sabda Manjari 1961 Ed – Reprint - 2013 – RS Vadhyar & Sons, Palghat.
- Swami Devarupananda – मन्त्रपुष्पम् - 4th – 2010 – Ramakrishna Math, Khar, Mumbai.
- Swami Paramarthananda – Aitareya Upanishad Discourse – 1st – 2015 – Arsha Avinash Foundation, Coimbatore.
- Sri Sri Ravi Shankar - Upanishad Vol1 - Ishavasya Kena Katha Yogasara - 1st – 2017 – Sri Sri Publications Trust, Bangalore.
- Ashwini Kumar Aggarwal – Dhatupatha of Panini – 2nd – 2017 – Devotees of Sri Sri Ravi Shankar Ashram, Punjab

# Epilogue

Festivals and Families are the backbone of society. Nature intervenes to re-establish this fabric.

Yoga, Pranayama, and Meditation coupled with Ayurveda and family Tradition make a perfect setup.

सर्वे भवन्तु सुखिनः । सर्वे सन्तु निरामयाः ।
सर्वे भद्राणि पश्यन्तु । मा कश्चिद् दुःख भाग्भवेत् ॥
ॐ शान्तिः शान्तिः शान्तिः ॥

When faith has blossomed in life,
Every step is led by the Divine.

Sri Sri Ravi Shankar

**Om Namah Shivaya**

जय गुरुदेव

www.ingramcontent.com/pod-product-compliance
Lightning Source LLC
LaVergne TN
LVHW091556170726
843492LV00007B/2159